TRAJECTORIES OF PHYSICAL AGGRESSION
FROM TODDLERHOOD
TO MIDDLE CHILDHOOD:
PREDICTORS, CORRELATES, AND OUTCOMES

NICHD Early Child Care Research Network

WITH COMMENTARY BY
William F. Arsenio

Willis F. Overton
Series Editor

MONOGRAPHS OF THE SOCIETY FOR RESEARCH IN CHILD DEVELOPMENT

Serial No. 278, Vol. 69, No. 4, 2004

 **Blackwell Publishing**

Boston, Massachusetts   Oxford, United Kingdom

TRAJECTORIES OF PHYSICAL AGGRESSION FROM TODDLERHOOD TO MIDDLE CHILDHOOD: PREDICTORS, CORRELATES, AND OUTCOMES

CONTENTS

COMMENTARY

ABSTRACT

Maternal reports of physical aggression from 24 months to third grade were examined in a diverse sample of over 1,100 children participating in the NICHD Study of Early Child Care and Youth Development. Most children showed low levels of aggression that declined over time. A person-centered analysis identified five aggression trajectories: two low-aggression trajectories and three trajectories characterized by at least moderate aggression at some point between 24 months and third grade. One trajectory group evidenced moderate aggression at 24 months that declined steeply; another showed modest aggression at 24 months that remained elevated at third grade. The fifth and smallest trajectory group showed high and stable aggression. Higher levels of family resources and more sensitive parenting predicted low levels of aggression, whereas higher sociodemographic risk and less sensitive, involved parenting, assessed from infancy through third grade, predicted higher and more stable aggression. Child-care parameters were not systematically related to aggression trajectories. Higher trajectories of aggression predicted poorer social and academic outcomes in third grade, whereas aggression evident in toddlerhood that declined by school entry was not associated with problematic functioning in third grade. Children in the two higher aggression trajectories also differed from one another in the type and severity of their problems in third grade. Some of these findings were confirmed when variable-centered data analyses were conducted. However, the person-centered analysis identified subgroups of children whose trajectories of aggression were obscured in the variable-centered analysis. Results indicate that not all aggressive toddlers are necessarily on a high-risk pathway; the course of aggression through early childhood is an important predictor of outcomes in middle childhood, and physical aggression tends to be more stable in the context of family adversity. Distinctions are drawn between normative, age-related aggressive behavior, and problematic aggression that emerges in early childhood.

I. INTRODUCTION

Interest in the early emergence and developmental course of aggression and related externalizing behavior in children is due in part to concerns about the stability of aggression from early to later childhood (Coie & Dodge, 1998; Huesmann, Eron, Lefkowitz, & Walder, 1984; Olweus, 1979; Patterson, DeBarshye, & Ramsey, 1989). This interest also stems from the well-established finding that early and persistent aggression is associated with other negative outcomes including poor emotion regulation and impulsive behavior, school failure and school drop-out, peer problems, and adolescent delinquency (Fergusson, Lynskey, & Horwood, 1996; Huesmann et al., 1984; Loeber, Farrington, Stouthamer-Loeber, Moffitt, & Caspi, 1998; Moffitt, 1993; Parker & Asher, 1987; Patterson et al., 1989; Tremblay, 2000). Thus, it has been argued that there is a large cost to society when children at risk for serious and persistent aggression are not identified early (e.g., Loeber & Farrington, 2000; Tremblay, 2000).

These concerns have fueled research tracing the developmental pathways from early aggression to later outcomes. Longitudinal studies have identified young children at risk of developing externalizing problems before school entry because of family risk (Belsky, Woodworth, & Crnic, 1996; Shaw, Owens, Vondra, Keenan, & Winslow, 1996; Spieker, Larson, Lewis, Keller, & Gilchrist, 1999), child characteristics (Bates, Dodge, Pettit, & Ridge, 1998; Campbell, Pierce, March, Ewing, & Szumowski, 1994; Richman, Stevenson, & Graham, 1982), or the interaction between family risk and child temperament (Bates et al., 1998; Belsky, Hsieh, & Crnic, 1998). These studies indicate that externalizing problems that include aggressive, disruptive, and noncompliant behaviors are reasonably stable and that some children who show high levels of early aggression and defiance have continuing problems, especially in the context of family adversity (Campbell, Shaw, & Gilliom, 2000).

Despite these concerns, aggressive behavior is also common in early childhood, and it shows a marked decline over the course of early development (Hartup, 1974; Tremblay, 2000), suggesting a normative function

1

for aggression in some social contexts. Tremblay and colleagues (Cote, Tremblay, Nagin, Zoccolillo, & Vitaro, 2002; Tremblay, 2000) argue that whereas toddlers commonly use physical aggression to settle disputes with peers over toys or to express anger, with the development of emotion regulation skills and the emergence of alternative strategies to deal with conflict, physical aggression becomes relatively rare. Brownell and Hazen (1999) have similarly argued that toddlers may use aggression to initiate playful interaction, but with the development of social and social-cognitive competence, such strategies are replaced by more mature social-communicative skills. By school entry, most children's language and cognitive abilities facilitate the use of alternative strategies: children negotiate to solve disputes, seek adult intervention, or use more subtle types of aggression such as arguing, name-calling, or social exclusion (Coie & Dodge, 1998; Crick, Casas, & Nelson, 2002; Hartup, 1996; Rubin, Bukowski, & Parker, 1998). Only a small number of children, mostly boys, continue to show much physical aggression toward peers or adults. Thus, in contrast to studies reporting that early individual differences in aggression are reasonably stable in extreme groups of high-risk children (e.g., Nagin & Tremblay, 1999; Shaw et al., 1996), others indicate that average levels of aggression and defiance decline with age during the second and third years of life, and that most children are reasonably compliant, cooperative, and prosocial by the time they enter school (Coie & Dodge, 1998; Hartup, 1996; Tremblay, 2000).

How does one reconcile these differing views of the development of aggressive and disruptive behavior? This question underscores two different perspectives that inform the study of social development including the development of aggression: a focus on individual differences and a focus on normative developmental change. Both are consistent with the findings of normative declines in aggressive behavior for most children, while many children may also retain the same rank order over time. However, studies also show that a small group of children can be identified who do not show normative declines in levels of aggression; indeed, their aggression remains well above normal levels across development, placing them at serious risk for adjustment difficulties in middle childhood, adolescence, and even young adulthood (e.g., Brame, Nagin, & Tremblay, 2001; Broidy, Nagin, Tremblay, Bates, Brame, Dodge, Fergusson, Horwood, Loeber, Laird, Lynam, Moffitt, Pettit, & Vitaro, 2003). Thus, one task for developmentalists is to differentiate young children with normative levels of aggressive behavior that declines as more adaptive social skills emerge, from young children whose relatively stable aggression is not replaced by developmentally more appropriate social skills, and is likely to remain at high and problematic levels. Recent studies have utilized person-centered techniques to identify children showing different patterns of aggressive behavior over

2

time in an attempt to address this issue (e.g., Brame et al., 2001; Broidy et al., 2003; Nagin & Tremblay, 1999; Shaw, Gilliom, Ingoldsby, & Nagin, 2003).

Person-centered approaches are used to identify conceptually distinct subsets of individuals, selected on the basis of behavioral characteristics or personality dimensions, on the assumption that the subgroups are meaningful, that individuals within a subgroup are relatively homogeneous, and that the subgroups differ from one another in important ways, consistent with theory (e.g., Bergman & Magnusson, 1997). Moreover, understanding something about the different categories of persons identified with person-centered methods should provide information that complements more traditional variable-centered methods and that may be obscured when all participants in a study are considered together (Bergman & Magnusson, 1997). Person-centered analyses are often based on typologies derived from patterns of behavior assessed at one point in time (e.g., Bergman & Magnusson, 1997; Hart, Atkins, & Fegley, 2003). For example, Hart et al. (2003) studied a large and diverse sample of preschool children participating in the National Longitudinal Study of Youth. Based on maternal ratings of personality traits, resilient, overcontrolled, and undercontrolled personality types were identified and the degree to which these types were associated with high versus low academic achievement and internalizing and externalizing problems was examined. The undercontrolled children had higher scores on externalizing behavior and lower academic achievement, both concurrently and over time; undercontrol also predicted declines in academic achievement. Of relevance to the current monograph, these authors identified subgroups or types of children with similar profiles at one point in time on personality measures and then examined whether the typology was a better predictor of functioning in other domains than individual trait measures.

An alternative way of identifying potentially homogeneous subgroups of children is to examine different patterns of change in the developmental course of a theoretically important behavior. Research on longitudinal patterns of change in aggression and antisocial behavior has been the focus of seminal research in developmental psychopathology (e.g., Cairns & Cairns, 1994; Loeber & Stouthamer-Loeber, 1998; Moffitt, 1993) because it is well documented that most children outgrow early problems, whereas a small subgroup appears to continue on a problematic developmental pathway (Moffitt, 1993). Thus, there has been an emphasis on longitudinal studies that identify subgroups of children with increasing or decreasing patterns of problem behavior (e.g., Campbell et al., 1994; Denham, Workman, Cole, Weissbrod, Kendziora, & Zahn-Waxler, 2000; Moffitt, Caspi, Dickson, Silva, & Stanton, 1996). Earlier person-centered research on problem children relied on cut-off scores or diagnoses that were consistent over time to identify subgroups (e.g., Campbell et al., 1994; Moffitt et al., 1996). A more recent and potentially important analytic tool to facilitate research on specific developmental patterns of behavior is Nagin's semiparametric group-based trajectory analysis (Nagin, 1999; Nagin & Tremblay, 1999). Trajectory analysis examines patterns of a specific behavior over time on the assumption that there are subgroups of children showing different and theoretically meaningful patterns of behavior *longitudinally*; that is, the developmental course or *trajectory* of the behavior, in this case aggression, defines subtypes showing different developmental histories, not only on the behavior in question, but on a range of child characteristics and environmental correlates of importance for understanding adjustment. Thus low, increasing, decreasing, or chronic patterns of aggression should be important predictors of later adjustment and also have different family correlates.

In the current report, we examine pathways of aggressive behavior in a large sample of children followed from infancy to middle childhood. Children in the sample are relatively diverse, but they cannot be characterized as at high risk for aggression or other negative outcomes. We use person-centered techniques to differentiate normative, age-related changes in aggression from potentially problematic levels of aggressive behavior assessed from early to middle childhood. Once patterns of aggression are identified, we also examine their antecedents and concurrent correlates to better understand potential processes associated with both declines in aggression and with the onset and maintenance of aggressive behaviors. Finally, we consider the implications of differing developmental patterns of aggressive behavior for the development of social competence, behavior problems, and academic achievement in third grade.

Because this sample was studied from birth, we are uniquely positioned to examine family and child characteristics very early in life (i.e., from birth to 2 years) that predict membership in one or another trajectory group. We focus on conceptually identified risk factors that are presumed to foster high levels of non-normative aggression and on conceptually derived positive or promotive factors presumed to support young children's development (Masten & Coatsworth, 1998; Gutman, Sameroff, & Cole, 2003; Sameroff, 2000). Promotive factors are distinguished from protective factors because they support children's development, regardless of level of risk (e.g., Sameroff, 2000) and thus, they may be associated either with consistently low aggression or with decreases in aggression to normative levels in early childhood. We also examine children's child-care history as a potential explanatory factor, as low-quality child care and/or many hours in child care may be associated with higher levels of aggressive behavior (Love, Harrison, Sagi-Schwartz, van IJzendoorn, Ross, Ungerer, Raikes, Brady-Smith, Boller, Brooks-Gunn, Constantine, Kisker, Paulsell, & Chanzan-Cohen, 2003; NICHD ECCRN, 2003a, b).

4

First, we review the literature on different patterns of early aggressive behavior and the implications of early-identified aggression for later functioning. Longitudinal studies that use person-centered approaches are emphasized. Next, we discuss both risk factors for aggression and promotive factors in the child and the child's environment that are usually associated with more positive functioning. Other issues to be discussed in this review include the definition and assessment of aggressive behavior at different ages. We also consider which outcomes of aggression need to be investigated to better understand its longitudinal course.

STUDIES OF SUBTYPES AND TRAJECTORIES OF AGGRESSION AND RELATED BEHAVIORS

Subtypes of Aggressive and Disruptive Behavior

Although some researchers have emphasized the stability of aggressive behavior (e.g., Olweus, 1979), a growing body of research on aggressive and antisocial behavior has focused on individual differences in aggression, including differing patterns of aggressive behavior over time. Thus, some studies have tested the assumption that although aggression is, on average, reasonably stable when examined with correlational techniques, not all aggressive children show persistent problems with aggressive or even externalizing behavior. A number of researchers have used conceptually derived cut-off scores or diagnostic criteria to identify subgroups of children, usually boys, who were expected to follow different developmental pathways of disruptive behavior over time. This attempt to identify meaningful subtypes of children, then, represents a person-centered approach. In general, the research suggests that for a few children, early aggression, especially when it is intense and frequent, may be a sign of emerging problems (Campbell, 1995, 2002; Tremblay, 2000).

To address the long-term implications of early aggression, we need to know about the immediate context of the child's aggression (is she/he with peers? Does the aggression seem to be provoked or not?), as well as its persistence over the short term (is it a *usual* reaction to peer conflict or parental limit-setting?), and about the childrearing and family context more generally, both concurrently and over time. This is because serious and persistent aggression is more likely when problem behavior in toddlerhood and the preschool period shows some degree of stability across settings and relationships (Campbell, 1995, 2002; Richman et al., 1982) and occurs in the context of family and psychosocial risk (e.g., Campbell, 2002; Coie & Dodge, 1998; Patterson et al., 1989; Shaw, Winslow, Owens, Vondra,

Cohn, & Bell, 1998; Tremblay, Pihl, Vitaro, & Dobkin, 1994). For example, parents who are harsh and/or inconsistent and also show poor affect regulation may model and/or reinforce less skillful social behavior in their young children (e.g., Patterson et al., 1989; Shaw et al., 1998). Persistent aggressive behavior in young children also occurs most often in tandem with other problems such as impulsivity and hyperactivity that reflect more general difficulties with behavioral control and emotion regulation (Calkins, 1994; Campbell, 2002; Denham et al., 2000; Rubin, Burgess, Dwyer, & Hastings, 2003), and these difficulties are more likely to be maintained in environments characterized by harsh control, and that also lack parental scaffolding and direction for more skillful social behavior with others (Cole, Teti, & Zahn-Waxler, 2003; Denham et al., 2000; Rubin et al., 2003). Thus, prediction is enhanced when multiple ecological factors surrounding the young child's aggression are considered.

Although they are intriguing, these findings need to be interpreted cautiously because bidirectional influences between an explosive child and less skilled parents are likely to be relevant to understanding the processes that facilitate the development of persistent aggression and related problem behaviors (e.g., Belsky et al., 1996; Campbell, Pierce, Moore, Marakovitz, & Newby, 1996; Shaw et al., 1998). These associations may reflect child–environment interactions (e.g., Bates et al., 1998; Belsky et al., 1998) related to child temperament and the nature of parenting. For example, more active, explosive and poorly regulated children may have parents who themselves are more excitable and disorganized, and thus, less able to set firm, consistent, and age-appropriate limits. Studies linking harsh parenting with children's problem behavior are consistent, but they also raise problems of interpretation because causal processes have not been identified unequivocally.

Despite these limitations, a number of studies have selected groups of young children at risk for persistent aggression and noncompliance and studied them over the course of early development to identify predictors of time-limited and stable behavior problems. For example, Campbell and her colleagues identified hard-to-manage preschool boys at age 4 on the basis of parent and teacher reports and followed them until they were 9 years old (Campbell, 1994; Campbell et al., 1996; Pierce, Ewing, & Campbell, 1999). The subgroup identified as showing persistent problems based on cut-off scores on maternal and other reports (father and/or teacher) at school entry was also found to have more problems with self-regulation when observed in the laboratory on measures of delay of gratification and resistance to temptation, and when observed interacting with peers in preschool. These boys came from families experiencing more stress than children with early but transient behavioral difficulties as identified by mothers and/or preschool teachers. Mothers of boys with persistent problems also behaved

6

more harshly when observed interacting with their preschool boys in a laboratory clean-up task at age 4; negative maternal behavior observed in the laboratory also predicted continuing problems at age 9, even after controlling for the level of initial problems and a concurrent indicator of harsh parenting (Campbell et al., 1994, 1996).

More recently, Denham et al. (2000) studied children with elevated disruptive behavior at age 4. Using cluster analytic methods, a person-centered technique, they identified a small group of children who were persistently disruptive over a 2-year period. These children were distinguished from those with early but improved problems by their experiences of lower levels of proactive parenting and higher levels of parental negative affect. These data were interpreted as suggesting that the observed maternal behavior did not support emotion regulation and the control of disruptive and aggressive behavior, although other interpretations are also possible as noted above.

Using data from the Dunedin, New Zealand birth cohort, Moffitt et al. (1996) studied boys from early childhood (age 3) to adolescence (age 18) and identified several distinct patterns of aggressive and antisocial behavior. Because boys were classified into distinct subgroups on the basis of patterns of behavior, this approach can also be considered person-centered. Some boys were identified as showing aggressive behavior in early and middle childhood, but not in adolescence. A second group was identified as showing aggressive and antisocial behavior only in adolescence; their aggressive behavior was deemed "adolescence-limited" and was considered to be developmentally normative. A third group, "life-course persistent," received elevated ratings from parents and teachers across childhood and the boys themselves reported engaging in delinquent behaviors in adolescence. Finally, some boys were consistently low in aggression.

Moffitt et al. (1996) then identified a number of personality and family variables that differentiated the life-course persistent, adolescence-limited, the childhood-only aggressive groups from one another. Children in the persistently aggressive group were observed to be more difficult and uncooperative with an examiner during an assessment at age 3. Over the course of development, the boys with childhood onset and persistent problems were distinguished from the other groups by their cognitive and language deficits, impulsivity, family adversity, and poor parenting. In adolescence, boys in the persistently antisocial group rated themselves as more impulsive, more alienated from their families, and less socially connected to others than boys in the adolescence-limited and no aggression groups, and they were also more likely to drop out of school.

Using data from the Minnesota High Risk Study, Aguilar, Sroufe, Egeland, and Carlson (2000) also examined outcomes of varying aggression

7

trajectories through age 16 in a sample followed from birth. They likewise used cut-off scores to establish theoretically meaningful subgroups differing in aggression and antisocial behavior. From the original 287 subjects, 120 were followed and classified into four groups based on scores obtained from parents, teachers, and the adolescents themselves from kindergarten to grade 6 and at age 16: early onset antisocial; late onset antisocial; early onset but not persistent; and no problems. Because the sample was high risk, 32% were rated as showing persistent problems whereas only 11% showed problems that started early and then declined. Numerous biological and contextual variables were examined, but the groups were most clearly differentiated by early psychosocial risk including poverty and single parenthood, and by child neglect and family stress in middle childhood. Children with early problems that were still evident in adolescence experienced consistently high levels of family and parenting risk. These findings are intriguing but they are limited by the relatively small and unique sample and high rate of sample attrition, as well as the large number of variables examined. However, consistent with other work, they implicate high levels of family stress in the persistence of aggression and related problems over the course of early development.

Other work has also emphasized the identification of children with problems that are apparent in early childhood and persist into adolescence (Patterson et al., 1989; Shaw, Bell, & Gilliom, 2000). For example, Patterson et al. (1989) have discussed "early starters" who begin showing aggressive and disruptive behavior in early childhood and progress through annoying and noncompliant behavior and fights with peers to more serious problems in adolescence. Loeber, Tremblay, Gagnon, and Charlebois (1989) identified boys whose above-average levels of aggression decreased over childhood (desistors) in contrast to those whose aggression persisted. Taken together, these studies indicate that several important and meaningful subgroups of children can be identified using a variety of person-centered approaches, including a group showing only normative or no aggressive behavior, and possibly three aggression groups: (a) a group that shows early aggression that diminishes over time (desistors), (b) a group that is low in aggression initially but increases over time (late starters or adolescence-limited), and (c) a high and stable group (life course persistent or early starters). The use of cut-off scores to identify homogeneous subgroups has been fruitful and has yielded many important findings that have influenced the current conceptualizations of the nature and course of externalizing behavior problems. However, the recent appearance of powerful analytic tools for examining longitudinal data (e.g., trajectory analysis, Nagin, 1999) allows for a more sophisticated assessment of trajectories of externalizing behavior than has been used in earlier studies.

8

Trajectories of Aggressive and Disruptive Behavior Over Time

Nagin and Tremblay (1999) were the first to introduce the person-centered semiparametric methodology to developmental psychologists and developmental psychopathologists. In this approach, scores on selected behaviors are modeled longitudinally to describe the developmental course of behavior among different latent classes or subgroups of children who show different patterns of change in the relevant behaviors over time (Nagin, 1999). Conceptually, this statistical approach is somewhat like cluster analysis in that the goal is a person-centered one of identifying groups of individuals who show homogeneous patterns of change over time on the behaviors of interest. The number of anticipated clusters is specified a priori and individual and group growth curves are estimated for the specific clusters. The model is based on the assumption that the population of children is composed of distinct groups of individuals who show different developmental trajectories of the target behavior, and that the individuals within each trajectory group are homogeneous in terms of their developmental patterns. As with diagnostic categories or clusters, all individuals in a particular trajectory group are viewed as equivalent, based on the argument that variation within a trajectory group is less informative than differences between trajectory groups. This approach has proven useful in describing general longitudinal patterns of behavior displayed by groups of children as well as each individual's deviation from these patterns, thus integrating the two primary goals of developmental research—the study of normative change and the study of individual differences.

Using this individual growth curve technique, Nagin and Tremblay (1999) examined the developmental trajectories of physical aggression in a sample of 1,037 French-speaking boys living in low-income neighborhoods of Montreal and considered to be at risk for externalizing behavior problems. Boys' behavior was rated by teachers at ages 6, 10, 11, 12, 13, 14, and 15 years of age on a three-item index of *physical* aggression, a five-item index of oppositional behavior, and a two-item index of hyperactivity. Although the focus of this study was on physical aggression, these other behaviors were also examined because they are part of the overall picture of externalizing problems and because the combination of aggression, defiance, and hyperactivity is often considered as a set of co-occurring risk factors for a persistent problem pathway (Lahey, Waldman, & McBurnett, 1999; Loeber, Lahey, Green, & Kalb, 2000; Moffitt, 1990, 1993; Patterson, DeGarmo, & Knutson, 2000). The ratings of physical aggression were best described by four developmental trajectories: (a) a consistently low group who showed minimal aggression over the course of development, (b) a moderate and declining group whose level of aggression was close to zero by age 15, (c) a group that started out as relatively high in aggression but

9

then declined to only a modest level, and (d) a small group of boys who remained high on aggression across the entire 9-year period. The pattern of results was similar for ratings of oppositional behavior, albeit with a somewhat larger moderate and declining group, suggesting that some oppositional behavior is normative in this age range. Further, just under half the boys in the physical aggression group were also categorized in the high and stable opposition group.

Several points are important about these data: teachers did not view most boys as especially physically aggressive in either childhood or adolescence (roughly 70% were rated low) and only a small number of boys (4%) were viewed by teachers as consistently aggressive over time. Moreover, there was no evidence of an adolescence-limited group of physically aggressive boys, at least not one that emerged by age 15. In addition, most of the boys showing moderate levels of aggression at school entry and in middle childhood were no longer rated as physically aggressive by teachers at age 15. Nagin and Tremblay (1999) also examined how well trajectory membership predicted self-reported physical violence and serious delinquency at age 17. When teachers viewed boys' physical aggression as low or declining, the boys themselves reported only limited aggression and delinquency at age 17, whereas boys judged by teachers as chronically aggressive reported much higher levels of violence and delinquent behavior. Earlier trajectories of teacher-rated oppositional and hyperactive behavior were at best weak predictors of adolescents' self-reported delinquency and aggression, underscoring the salience of early *physical* aggression in predicting negative outcomes in adolescence. In addition, even within the high trajectory group, not all aggressive boys continued to report high levels of physical aggression in adolescence (Brame et al., 2001).

In a recent special issue of *Developmental Psychology* focused on *violent children*, Broidy et al. (2003) examined developmental trajectories of disruptive behavior from ages 6 or 7 until early adolescence in six different large and reasonably representative samples (including the sample from the Nagin and Tremblay, 1999 paper), two samples each studied in Canada, the United States, and New Zealand. These samples varied somewhat in level of risk, with risk being somewhat higher (either because the children were from low-income families or because they were oversampled for signs of disruptive behavior) in the Canadian samples and one U.S. sample; the two New Zealand samples were birth cohorts, not identified as at risk for behavior problems.

Across these six samples, teacher ratings of physical aggression were modeled using Nagin's (1999) methodology. Data for boys and girls were examined separately; only four samples included girls. Among the males, low and declining groups were identified, with roughly 90–95% showing relatively low levels of physical aggression by age 11, 12, or 13. In addition, in each sample a small and highly aggressive group was identified (from 4% to 11% of the sample); in some samples, this group showed stable and high teacher-reported aggression, whereas in the two U.S. samples, the level of teacher-reported aggression rose somewhat in the highest aggression subgroup. Among girls, teacher-reported physical aggression was generally much lower, but a stable aggression group was also identified in each sample. Although the rates of stable aggression ranged from 3% to 14% of the samples, the overall level of stable, teacher-reported physical aggression in girls was much lower than for boys, and the vast majority of girls showed very low to no physical aggression by adolescence. In one sample, a group of girls showing steep declines in teacher-reported aggressive behavior was also identified. It is noteworthy that across samples, relatively similar patterns of physical aggression were in evidence, that in each sample a small group of children showing persistent aggression was identified (even when the sample was not considered at risk for aggression), and that there was no indication of a group with low initial aggression that then increased even to moderate levels in adolescence.

As in the original Nagin and Tremblay (1999) study, two additional issues were addressed. First the authors assessed the degree to which these trajectories predicted self-reports of violent or non-violent delinquency in early (age 13, two samples) or late (age 17–18, three samples) adolescence. In all the samples, high levels of teacher-reported physical aggression across childhood predicted later self-reports of violent delinquency, especially in boys, with less consistent findings for girls. Moreover, high and stable levels of teacher-rated physical aggression also predicted self-reports of non-violent delinquency such as theft and vandalism. The link between early *physical* aggression as reported by teachers and later self-reported delinquency in boys remained even when other earlier indicators of teacher-reported disruptive behavior and hyperactivity were controlled, although oppositional behavior and non-aggressive conduct problems were also associated with delinquent outcomes for boys. These data are important in showing similar patterns of aggression over childhood and adolescence across six samples in three countries. At the same time, the relatively stable levels of aggression in the high trajectory groups, first studied at age 6, raise the question of *when* in development these behaviors emerged and highlight the need for studies that examine much earlier trajectories of aggressive behavior (Tremblay, 2000). The research presented in this monograph addresses this question.

To date, only one study has examined trajectories of aggressive and disruptive behavior in children prior to school entry using Nagin's (1999) clustering method. Importantly, when examining trajectories of aggressive behavior prior to school entry, the source of judgments about aggression shifts to mothers' reports. This may potentially yield higher numbers of

consistently high aggression groups because of the stability of the informant, and possibly the stability in contexts related to aggressive behavior.
Shaw, Gilliom, Ingoldsby, and Nagin (2003) examined trajectories underlying maternal reports of *conduct problems* (5 items assessing physical
aggression, disobedience, and temper tantrums) assessed 5 times from ages
2 to 8 in a sample of 284 boys from low-income families in the United States,
recruited from the Women, Infants, and Children (WIC) program. Results
were quite similar to those reported so far.

Four trajectories describing disruptive behavior were identified: (a) low
and declining, (b) moderate and declining, (c) high moderate and declining,
and (d) stable high. The low and declining group, representing 42% of the
sample, most likely reflects normative and typical physical aggression and
disobedience as reported by mothers. By age 8, only 6% of the sample was
characterized by stable and high disruptive behavior, according to maternal
reports. From a developmental perspective, it is interesting that three
groups showed a decline in mother-rated problem behavior, but that prior
to 5 years of age no group hovered at 0; this is likely because in toddlerhood
and the early preschool period, behaviors like temper tantrums and disobedience are fairly common and age-normative (see, e.g., Koot, 1993;
Koot, Van Den Oord, Verhulst, & Boomsma, 1997). Those boys in the stable
and high conduct problem group were rated by their mothers not only as
disobedient but also as aggressive to people and animals, again underscoring the important predictive role that severe and persistent physical aggression appears to play in identifying children at risk for more negative
outcomes in middle childhood and adolescence. The findings from this
study are quite consistent with the findings on older children and they
suggest that severe and persistent early aggression and disruptive behavior
may be a marker for more serious problems in middle childhood and adolescence. At the same time, it is obvious that the maintenance of aggressive
behavior can only be understood in the wider context of the child's family
and social environment (Bronfenbrenner, 1979).

Correlates of Trajectory Membership

The research on trajectories of behavior problems discussed so far has
focused on *descriptions* of pathways of aggressive behavior and on predic-
tions from these pathways to specific negative outcomes of violence and
delinquency. The emphasis has been on identifying consistent behavioral
trajectories across cohorts and then assessing the degree to which these
trajectories are themselves predictive of later aggressive and/or antisocial
behavior with a focus on within-child factors and behavioral continuity from
early aggression to later indices of aggressive and delinquent behavior. Little attention has yet been paid to family factors or child characteristics, other

than aggression, that might be associated with membership in a particular trajectory group. This is despite the data reviewed earlier, implicating family stress and harsh parenting as important predictors of continuing externalizing problems in highly disruptive groups of children (Aguilar et al., 2000; Campbell et al., 1996; Moffitt et al., 1996).

In one of the few studies addressing this issue in trajectory groups defined by longitudinal modeling of problem behavior, Nagin and Tremblay (2001) examined sociodemographic family risk factors, including family intactness, age of parents at child's birth, and parental education in their sample of low-income boys in Montreal studied from age 6 to 15. There were linear relationships between trajectory group membership based on teacher ratings of physical aggression (low, moderate-declining, high-declining, chronic) and these family characteristics. Boys were more likely to be on a persistent aggression pathway if they were raised in a single-parent household by a mother with low educational attainment (less than ninth grade) who had been a teenager at the time of their birth; only maternal age (being a young mother) and low maternal education discriminated between the high, but declining aggression group and the chronic aggression group. Boys whose very young mothers had dropped out of school were three times more likely to be in the chronic aggression group than in the high, but decreasing aggression group.

Shaw et al. (2003) used a set of observational measures obtained in infancy and toddlerhood to compare trajectory groups, defined on the basis of disruptive behavior from age 2 to 8, in their sample of low-income U.S. families. They identified several potential child, parenting, maternal, and demographic factors that they reasoned should predict membership in one of the high trajectory groups defined by maternal reports. These included high fearlessness (lack of inhibition) in the child observed in the laboratory at age 2, maternal rejecting parenting observed in the laboratory during a clean-up task at ages 18 months and 2 years, and maternal reports of depressive symptoms as well as maternal age and education level. Only fearlessness in early childhood and maternal depressive symptoms uniquely predicted trajectory membership, distinguishing between the two low or declining (low and declining; moderate and declining) and two higher (moderate and decreasing; high and stable) disruptive behavior problem groups; child fearlessness and maternal rejecting parenting differentiated between the two higher trajectory groups as well, with higher levels of fearlessness and rejecting parenting increasing the odds of being in the high and stable group of disruptive boys. Clearly, this work is provocative in suggesting that certain family risk factors paired with certain child characteristics predict membership in the more problematic groups. However, maternal reports of depressive symptoms and parental behavior may be somewhat confounded with maternal reports of disruptive behavior used to identify trajectories. Moreover, the bidirectional influence of fearlessness on rejecting parenting needs to be considered, along with the possibility that these links reflect, in part, genetic factors. Finally, a more thorough investigation of risk factors for early developing trajectory membership and of changes in risk factors over time are needed to elucidate the processes that may partially account for different pathways of aggressive behavior in children. We will address these issues in this study.

RISK FACTORS FOR AGGRESSION AND NEGATIVE OUTCOMES

The term "risk factor" originally emerged in epidemiological research aimed at identifying the causes of public health problems. Sameroff (2000) points out that the delineation of risk factors is an exercise in establishing probabilities rather than causes because any single risk factor or combination of risk factors has only probabilistic associations with the outcome of interest. Over the past several decades of research in developmental psychopathology, many conceptual models and empirical studies have emphasized risk factors in the child, family, and wider community that appear to increase the likelihood or *risk* of negative child outcomes (e.g., Masten & Coatsworth, 1998; Patterson et al., 1989; Rutter, 1979; Sameroff, Seifer, Baldwin, & Baldwin, 1993; Werner & Smith, 1977). Risk factors have been examined as correlates and predictors of a variety of child and adolescent outcomes including poorer cognitive and language development (e.g., Burchinal, Roberts, Hooper, & Zeisel, 2000; Duncan, Brooks-Gunn, & Klebanov, 1994; Sameroff et al., 1993), poor psychosocial adjustment and the emergence of behavior problems (e.g., Duncan et al., 1994; Moffitt, 1993; Patterson et al., 1989; Shaw et al., 1998), and more serious, even diagnosable, levels of psychopathology in children (e.g., Campbell et al., 1996; Lavigne, Arend, Rosenbaum, Binns, Christoffell, & Gibbons, 1998; Moffitt et al., 1996; Shaw et al., 1996). In general, a host of similar risk factors has been identified, regardless of the outcome, although some attempts have been made to search for more specific risk factors for particular outcomes (e.g., Deater-Deckard, Dodge, Bates, & Pettit, 1998; Greenberg, Lengua, Coie, Pinderhughes, Bierman, Dodge, Lochman, & McMahon, 1999). Furthermore, similar sets of risk factors have been identified in clinical samples, high-risk samples, and population-based, epidemiological samples (e.g., Conduct Problem Prevention Research Group, 1999; Fergusson et al., 1996; Greenberg et al., 1999; Lahey et al., 1999; Loeber et al., 1998; Moffitt et al., 1996, 2001).

Following from Bronfenbrenner's (1979) ecological model, there is general agreement that risk factors can be conceptualized in terms of

14

sociodemographic characteristics of families (e.g., parental occupation and educational level, marital status and family structure, family finances, poverty, ethnicity), particular child characteristics (e.g., difficult temperament, cognitive or language delays), more proximal family characteristics such as parent–child relationships and childrearing (e.g., low warmth, harsh discipline, rejection), family relationships and family climate (e.g., parental depression or other psychopathology, family conflict, low social support, high stress), and more distal factors such as neighborhood and community characteristics (e.g., quality of child care centers and schools, neighborhood safety). These and other risk factors have been identified consistently and have linked to problematic outcomes in scores of studies (e.g., Bradley, Mundfrom, Whiteside, Casey, & Barrett, 1994; Burchinal et al., 2000; Campbell, 2002; Cummings, Davies, & Campbell, 2000; Greenberg et al., 1999; Liaw & Brooks-Gunn, 1994; Rutter, 1979; Sameroff et al., 1993; Shaw et al., 1996).

Despite the overall agreement on the importance of risk factors, debate continues on how best to conceptualize the construct of risk (Burchinal et al., 2000; Deater-Deckard et al., 1998; Greenberg et al., 1999) because it has also been well established that particular risk factors tend to co-occur (Burchinal et al., 2000; Sameroff et al., 1993) and that negative outcomes are associated with a convergence of risk, not with one or two isolated risk factors. Furthermore, the task remains to identify those risk factors that are relatively specific to particular negative outcomes as well as those that are more generic. The actual causal processes by which particular factors convey risk are also the subject of some debate and current research (e.g., Denham et al., 2000; Patterson et al., 2000). As with the identification of trajectories, there are both theoretical and methodological issues that come into play.

Much of the seminal risk research has been conducted using a cumulative risk factor model in which risk factors are dichotomized as high or low and then the total number of risk factors is related to particular negative outcomes (e.g., Forehand, Armistead, & David, 1997; Rutter, 1979; Sameroff et al., 1993; Shaw, Vondra, Dowdell-Hommerding, Keenan, & Dunn, 1994). In general, results indicate that children with more risk factors have more negative outcomes, although some studies suggest the possibility of a threshold effect (e.g., Forehand et al., 1997; Rutter, 1979) whereby risk emerges only when a certain number of risk factors are present. For example, Rutter (1979) identified six risk factors as a marker of a particularly high level of risk for poor developmental outcomes, whereas children with fewer than six risk factors appeared better able to weather adversity. At the conceptual level, however, it seems logical that certain risk factors should be more predictive of particular negative outcomes than others and that collapsing across multiple risks may obscure the processes that account for associations between specific risk factors and specific outcomes.

15

The goal of risk research is not only to identify markers of risk but also to delineate mechanisms that explain why specific risk factors have negative sequelae for the child. Studies linking harsh, punitive, and rejecting parenting with children's externalizing problems have been particularly fruitful in identifying specific pathways by which parenting appears to facilitate aggressive and noncompliant behavior in children (e.g., Patterson et al., 1989, 2000; Kilgore, Snyder, & Lentz, 2000). First, negative parenting serves as a model for aggressive behavior with siblings and peers (e.g., Strassberg, Dodge, Pettit, & Bates, 1994). Second, negative, punitive parenting tends to exacerbate coercive cycles that fuel parent–child conflict and child noncompliance (e.g., Belsky et al., 1996; Denham et al., 2000; Kilgore et al., 2000; Shaw et al., 1998). Thus, it seems reasonable to suppose, as these studies have demonstrated, that negative parenting serves as a specific risk factor for externalizing behavior in children. Intervention studies also provide support for the argument that punitive and harsh parenting, at least partially, determines increases in aggressive and noncompliant behavior (Cowan & Cowan, 2002; Patterson, Reid, & Dishion, 1992).

Similarly, the absence of positive parenting reflected in low warmth, sensitivity, and responsiveness has been linked with aggressive behavior and noncompliance (e.g., Denham et al., 2000; Pettit, Laird, Dodge, Bates, & Criss, 2001), presumably because a strong parent–child relationship facilitates socialization including learning to cooperate and share, and learning to regulate negative emotions including anger (Denham et al., 2000; Eisenberg & Fabes, 1998; Kochanska, 1997; Maccoby & Martin, 1983). Sociodemographic risks have also been identified in many studies (e.g., Conger, Wallace, Sun, Simons, McLoyd, & Brody, 2002; Deater-Deckard et al., 1998; Greenberg et al., 1999). These may operate both directly, e.g., by exposing children to stress, and indirectly through the impact of poverty and family stress on parental warmth and involvement (Greenberg et al., 1999; McLoyd, 1990, 1998), as it has been well established that parents who are themselves preoccupied with daily stresses of making ends meet or finding a job are less patient and warm with their children (Belsky, 1984; Conger et al., 2002; McLoyd, 1990, 1998).

The challenge of studying which risk factors are most important, whether specific risk factors predict specific outcomes, and then delineating the processes by which risk factors operate has been highlighted in several recent articles. In particular, Burchinal et al. (2000) compared the strengths and weaknesses of three different approaches to studying risk. Because it is well known that risks operate together rather than individually, it is difficult to disentangle, e.g., the effects of sociodemographic risk from the effects of more proximal risks associated with family relations and styles of caregiving. This means that by definition, risks of interest are often highly correlated with one another.

Burchinal et al. (2000) selected a set of nine sociodemographic and caregiving risk factors that have been identified in previous research to predict cognitive and language development in high-risk samples (Bradley & Caldwell, 1984; Liaw & Brooks-Gunn, 1994; Sameroff et al., 1993). These were then examined as predictors of children's cognitive and language development from 12 to 48 months in a sample of low-income, African American mothers, most of whom were single. Risk factors were analyzed using standard multiple regression techniques with each risk factor entered independently and as a risk index in which risk factors were dichotomized and then the number of risk factors determined. Although individual risk factors considered together accounted for more variance in preschool outcomes than did the risk index, because of the correlated nature of the risk factors, few individual risk factors were identified as unique predictors of outcome in longitudinal analyses. This paper underscores the complex issues surrounding analysis of risk factor data as well as the fact that different approaches to analysis can lead to different conclusions. Therefore, in the current paper we examined both conceptually related sets of risk factors and a cumulative risk index.

Several other recent studies have examined how well individual and multiple risk factors predict externalizing problems in children over time, and thus, are directly relevant to some of the issues considered in this *Monograph*. Greenberg et al. (1999) used data from the Fast Track Intervention comparison group, and examined 13 risk factors, assessed at the end of kindergarten and grouped into socio-demographic, family, and neighborhood risk to predict social and academic outcomes at the end of first grade. Family risk variables accounted for unique variance in both mother and teacher ratings of externalizing behavior over and above the effects of demographic variables. In particular, stressful life events and negative emotional expression in the family were the most consistent predictors of teacher ratings of noncompliance and poor concentration, underscoring the unique contribution of proximal family variables to children's externalizing behavior in the early school years.

In yet another study, both individual risk factors within specific domains and a cumulative risk index for each domain were examined as predictors of parent and teacher ratings of externalizing problems and peer ratings of aggression from ages 5–10 (Deater-Deckard et al., 1998). Risk factors were assessed prior to kindergarten entry and categorized as either child risk (e.g., difficult temperament, medical problems), sociocultural risk (poverty, single parent household), parenting and family risk (e.g., exposure to violence, harsh discipline, amount of child care), or negative peer experiences (e.g., peer rejection). The question was whether each domain of risk contributed uniquely to the prediction of externalizing problems and aggression and also whether specific risks or cumulative risk within each domain accounted for the most variance in outcomes. Three competing models were tested: the first stipulates that risk domains are essentially redundant with one another given their correlations and that one risk factor may set off a process leading to other risks. For example, children who are irritable and uncooperative may elicit harsh discipline; sociocultural risks are strongly associated with harsh discipline, and so they do not provide additional information when both are included in analyses. The second model proposes that multiple domains of risk converge, but they are each important in the development of problems. Finally, the third model assumes that cumulative risk is operative and that it is the number of risks that contributes to overall stress rather than specific risks that matter.

These models were tested with data from 585 families participating in the Child Development Project (Deater-Deckard et al., 1998). Results indicated that each domain of risk factors predicted the three externalizing outcomes, and overall they accounted for from 36% to 45% of the variance. In contrast, the cumulative risk index accounted for 20–30% of the variance. Consistent with the papers discussed earlier, information from individual risk factors within domains tended to explain larger proportions of the variance in outcomes, although overlap among risk factors meant that the unique variance accounted for by individual predictors was often small. Taken together, these studies suggest that the amount of nonspecific risk matters, but that individual risk factors convey important information that is lost in cumulative risk indices. Moreover, the study of specific risk factors within conceptually derived domains of risk provides clues about the causal mechanisms that may account for the links between specific indicators of risk and problem outcomes. We examine a number of similar risk factors in the current study, both as individual predictors of trajectory membership and as part of a cumulative risk index.

PROTECTION AND PROMOTION OF POSITIVE DEVELOPMENTAL OUTCOMES IN CHILDREN AT RISK FOR PROBLEM BEHAVIOR

Developmental psychopathology focuses on the roots of competence as well as the roots of disorder (Masten & Coatsworth, 1995), thereby incorporating a focus on positive influences on development, as well as on risk factors. Many studies highlight the importance of a positive childrearing environment for good adjustment (see Luthar, Cicchetti, & Becker, 2000a; Maccoby & Martin, 1983) and studies of normal development focus primarily on positive influences (e.g., Kochanska, 1997; Maccoby & Martin, 1983). However, in the developmental psychopathology area, the emphasis has been on risk factors and abnormal development, and positive influences, although recognized, have not been as clearly conceptualized or as thoroughly investigated. This is partly because individuals who showed positive adaptation in the presence of risk were once considered atypical and received little research attention. Eventually they became the subject of inquiry in their own right, and the field of resilience research was initiated (e.g., Garmezy, 1974). The concept of protective factors was used to explain the positive developmental outcomes of resilient individuals who were reared under various conditions of adversity.

Although Rutter (1987) argued for a strict use of the term "protective factors" such that they are meaningful only in the context of risk, many researchers have used the term more broadly, to discuss both main-effects models and interaction processes (see Gutman et al., 2003; Luthar et al., 2000a). Furthermore, most studies have defined protective or promotive factors as the extreme positive pole of the same dimensional variables that define risk at the extreme negative pole (Stouthamer-Loeber, Loeber, Farrington, Zhang, Van Kammen, & Maguin, 1993). This makes it difficult to maintain the distinction between risk factors and protective factors (Sameroff, 2000), a concern that poses a distinct challenge for identifying and understanding factors related to the development and maintenance of problem behavior and its counterpart in prosocial functioning. Sameroff (2000), in attempting to preserve the strict interpretation of protective factors, suggested that a better term for positive influences that benefit all children is promotive factors. Sameroff, Bartko, Baldwin, Baldwin, and Seifer (1998) reported that summing promotive factors essentially results in findings that are the mirror image of findings related to summing risks. Not surprisingly, indices associated with successful adaptation tend to cluster together (Carnegie Council on Adolescent Development, 1989) just as risk indices tend to cluster (Masten & Coatsworth, 1998).

Garmezy's (1993) review of stress-resistant children identified variables that have positive effects on children, including characteristics of the family and of external support systems such as teachers and peers. The research literature also suggests that particular child and family characteristics may buffer children from the negative effects of limited resources and family stress. These include an easy-going temperament and high IQ (Bates et al., 1998; Belsky et al., 1998; Denham et al., 2000; Masten, Hubbard, Gest, Tellegen, Garmezy, & Ramirez, 1999), improvements in financial status (Dearing, McCartney, & Taylor, 2001), maternal sensitivity and proactive parenting (Denham et al., 2000; Pettit, Bates, & Dodge, 1997), and in middle childhood, positive peer relationships (Criss, Pettit, Bates, Dodge, & Lapp, 2002). Certain child-care experiences also buffer the effects of limited family resources. Examples include the cognitive and behavioral benefits of high-quality child care for children in poverty (Caughy, DiPietro, & Strobino, 1994; Votruba-Drzal, Coley, & Chase-Lansdale, 2004). However, these positive characteristics and experiences should be associated with good adjustment regardless of risk status (Luthar, Cicchetti, & Becker, 2000b).

Just as with risk factors, the research challenge is to understand the processes that explain protective and promotive effects. Protective factors may operate in a number of complex ways, e.g., by providing children with compensatory relationships with parents or others that motivate them and steer them into adaptive activities, by serving as positive role models, and by allowing children to develop skills and competencies that in turn lead to school success and positive relationships with more prosocial children (Garmezy, 1993). However, it is also true that most children benefit from positive and warm parenting, positive peer relations, and so on. Thus, promotive factors, rather than protective factors as strictly defined may be relevant to outcomes because they operate in the same way at all levels of risk. In the current study, we examine some of these promotive factors, particularly as they relate to the decrease in aggressive behavior over time in children at especially high initial levels. For example, we include measures of maternal sensitivity and child-care quality that would be expected to be associated with positive functioning in children regardless of level of risk, and may also predict declines in aggressive behavior over time.

CHILD CARE AND AGGRESSION TRAJECTORIES

In the context of risk and promotive factors, we also address the association between features of early child-care experiences—specifically, amount, quality, and type—and *trajectories* of physical aggression. The NICHD Study of Early Child Care and Youth Development has followed a large and diverse national sample of children and families from birth and studied the amount, quality, and type of child care utilized from early infancy through 54 months. The NICHD Study was designed to address questions about the impact of the amount and quality of early child care on children's adjustment. One ongoing debate has focused on whether early and extensive child care is associated with elevated levels of aggression and other externalizing problems (see reviews in Belsky, 2001; NICHD ECCRN, 2003a), and also whether higher quality care may promote social skills, and thus, be associated with lower levels of aggression (NICHD ECCRN, 2003b). This debate has highlighted the need to take into account family background factors before attributing causal influence to any feature of child care and also the possibility that data linking amount and timing of child care with problem behavior are a function of low-quality care.

In an earlier paper from the NICHD Study examining the effects of quantity, quality, and type of child care, controlling for a host of family background characteristics, we reported that more hours in any kind of nonmaternal child care from infancy to 54 months, and more time spent in center care in particular, predicted higher ratings of externalizing problems generally, and aggression specifically, at 54 months and kindergarten (NICHD ECCRN, 2003a). These effects were more consistent and robust for caregiver and teacher ratings than for maternal ratings (NICHD ECRRN, 2003a). Importantly, the effect of hours in care remained significant when child care quality and family variables were controlled and, for the most part, quality of care was unrelated to externalizing problems at 54 months and in kindergarten, although lower quality was related to problem behavior assessed at 24 and 36 months (NICHD ECRRN, 1998).

In considering findings from the NICHD Study, it is important to note that the sample is diverse, but it is not a sample selected to be high risk or low income. This is noteworthy because two recent reports indicate that in high-risk, low-income samples amount of care interacts with child-care quality to predict adjustment. More specifically, Votruba-Drzal et al. (2004) reported that many hours in care of low quality was associated with higher levels of externalizing problems whereas many hours in high-quality care predicted lower levels of problem behavior for children whose mothers were in welfare to work programs. High-quality child care also served as a buffer in the context of family risk. In a second study that also focused on low-income children, Loeb, Fuller, Kagan, and Carrol (2004) found that low-quality care, especially in family day care homes, was associated with higher rates of behavior problems, whereas high-quality center care was not. Thus, these papers suggest that quantity, quality, and type of care matter in explaining the emergence of behavior problems for low-income children and thus, just as in our earlier work, all should be considered when examining aggression trajectories.

The current study addresses a different question about child care and aggression than our earlier report or the recent investigations just cited because the focus is on *trajectories* of physically aggressive behavior. That is, we use a person-centered approach to identify subgroups of children and then examine adjustment as a function of subgroup or trajectory membership, rather than looking at links between general levels of externalizing problems or aggression and outcomes (a variable-centered approach). Further, the focus is on physical aggression, rather than on externalizing behavior generally and on the developmental course of aggressive behavior, rather than aggression at any one point in time. We are also concerned exclusively with maternal reports of aggression. In this study, we ask whether the patterns or trajectories of physical aggression over time are predicted by different amounts of child care, by variations in the quality of child care, and/or by experience in center care either from infancy to toddlerhood (3–24 months) or through the preschool period (24–54 months).

21

Thus, many hours of care from early infancy and/or low-quality child care and/or center-care experience may be associated with a high and stable trajectory of aggressive behavior from 24 months to third grade, indicating that low quality care and many hours of early child care may be additional risk factors for a pattern of persistent aggressive behavior. Conversely, high-quality care may be associated with decreases in aggression for some aggressive children.

MEASUREMENT ISSUES AND OUTCOMES

The research literature on children's aggressive and disruptive behavior has utilized both parent and teacher reports and both have been found to be reliable and valid indicators of child adjustment (Achenbach, 1991), although there is only modest agreement between them (Achenbach, McConaughy, & Howell, 1987) except at the extremes of problematic behavior. This is partly because there is a degree of situational specificity to aggressive and disruptive behavior, as well as differences in expectations and thresholds across different reporters. In the studies of trajectories described earlier, most used teacher reports to assess physical aggression, but this work focused on school-age children. The one prior investigation to examine toddlers (Shaw et al., 2003) used maternal reports because not all children in the sample were in some form of out-of-home care for which teachers could provide ratings. In the current report focusing on aggression beginning in early childhood, we likewise examine maternal reports of aggressive behavior over time because not all children were in child care by 24 months (NICHD ECCRN, 1998). Similar to Shaw et al. (2003), we examine maternal ratings of aggressive and destructive behavior over time to establish trajectories of aggressive behavior from 24 months to third grade. The use of maternal reports may overestimate stability because, unlike the work examining teacher-reports, we are relying on the same informant over time, and family risk and maternal reports may also be confounded to some degree. However, this approach allows us to maximize the number of children with usable data over a 7-year period from 24 months to third grade when children were on average 9 years of age.

Most studies of trajectories of aggressive and disruptive behavior in children have examined delinquent outcomes in adolescence. Clear links have been demonstrated between high and stable trajectories of aggressive behavior across childhood and adolescence and later violent and non-violent delinquency (Broidy et al., 2003). Thus, outcome data have focused almost exclusively on continuity between earlier and later aggression, with aggression defined differently at later ages. However, early and persistent

22

aggression should predict a range of negative outcomes of varying levels of severity. Further, the focus only on serious delinquency overlooks the possibility that children with moderate and declining levels of aggression may also have difficulties in school or with peers, even if they do not ultimately report serious violence or delinquent behavior. Finally, research on younger samples followed to middle childhood and assessed on a broader range of adjustment outcomes may shed light on the processes by which stable aggressive behavior from toddlerhood to elementary school becomes entrenched in patterns that then lead to further escalating aggression in adolescence. Such work may also provide a clearer picture of the processes associated with declining aggression in middle childhood, evident in the earlier studies (Broidy et al., 2003), but little explored. With this in mind, we examined the degree to which aggression trajectory membership predicted a range of adjustment outcomes in third grade, including not only behavior problems but also academic and social competence, and functioning in the peer group.

SEX DIFFERENCES IN AGGRESSION

Most studies examining the trajectories of aggressive behavior have focused only on boys. Studies that include girls indicate that rates of aggressive behavior are substantially lower in girls than in boys in middle childhood and adolescence (Broidy et al., 2003). However, physical aggression in girls also predicts negative outcomes (Broidy et al., 2003). Although sex differences in aggression are well documented (Maccoby, 1998), there is debate in the literature about when they are first evident. For example, Keenan and Shaw (1997) argue that sex differences in aggression and disruptive behavior are not apparent in toddlerhood. In a recent short-term longitudinal study examining peer-directed aggression in toddlers, Hay, Castle, and Davies (2000) assessed the unprovoked use of force during play with familiar peers and distinguished between instrumental aggression aimed at obtaining a toy (grab) from physical aggression (hit) apparently meant to hurt the peer. No sex differences were found on either parent ratings of aggression or observations of peer play. Surprisingly, although the rates of grabbing toys declined considerably over the follow-up period from ages 18–24 months to 30 months of age, rates of physical aggression although initially lower, showed no decline. Moreover, aggression in girls as assessed with both observations and with mother-reports was more stable than in boys. This is not consistent with most research on aggression in girls' peer relations (Maccoby, 1998), but it highlights the need for more studies that examine the emergence and longitudinal course of physical aggression

23

in girls as well as boys. We include girls in the current study in an effort to shed light on this issue.

THE CURRENT STUDY

In the current report, we use data from the NICHD Study of Early Child Care and Youth Development to examine trajectories of aggressive behavior as rated by mothers from 24 months to third grade, analyzed using Nagin's group-based, semiparametric method (Nagin, 1999; Nagin & Tremblay, 1999). We expect that, similar to the report of Shaw et al. (2003), we will find at least four trajectories of aggression that include a consistently low group, a moderate and declining group, a high and declining group, and a consistently high group. Because we are not examining a sample selected to be at high sociodemographic risk, it is likely that a smaller proportion of children will be identified as showing consistently high aggression than found by Shaw et al. (2003). We also anticipate that more boys than girls will be identified in the moderate and high aggression trajectory groups.

In Chapter II, we describe the study methodology. In Chapter III, we report the results of the trajectory analyses of aggressive behavior. Next, in Chapter IV, we examine a large set of risk factors as predictors of trajectory membership, selected to be consistent with the risk factor framework discussed earlier and identified as important in prior research. Measures are derived from multiple sources and multiple methods including observations obtained in home, laboratory, and child care settings. Predictive data were collected when study children were 6, 15, and 24 months old, thereby predating the measures of aggression used to define trajectories. These include sociodemographic factors of maternal education, family income, and family composition (Burchinal et al., 2000; Liaw & Brooks-Gunn, 1994; Sameroff et al., 1993), family and parenting measures including the quality of the home environment (Bradley et al., 1994), maternal sensitivity and responsiveness (Sameroff et al., 1993), maternal attitudes toward childrearing, and maternal depressive symptoms (Burchinal et al., 2000; Sameroff et al., 1993), the child's cognitive functioning at 24 months, and the quality and amount of child care that the child experienced (Deater-Deckard et al., 1998; NICHD ECCRN, 2003a, b).

Our measures of children's functioning and social context index risk at one extreme and should be predictive of membership in one of the higher aggression groups. For example, we expect that living in a single-parent, low-income family during infancy will predict membership in a high aggression group, as will measures of maternal depressive symptoms, a less stimulating and responsive family environment, and less child-centered attitudes about childrearing. In addition, in Chapter IV, we include time-varying risk factors studied longitudinally that, theoretically, should be related to trajectory membership. For example, we expect that high levels of aggression over time will be associated with high and persistent measures of maternal depressive symptoms and with lower observed maternal sensitivity across the child's life, whereas changes in these risk indicators from early to middle childhood will predict membership in a trajectory group showing declining aggression scores. This approach should also permit us to examine the timing of risk more precisely, and the degree to which inflections in trajectories co-occur with changes in family and other risk factors.

In Chapter V, we examine the developmental sequelae of being in one of the trajectory groups and we focus on a range of social, achievement, and adjustment outcomes measured at third grade, most of which are independent of the assessments of aggression. These include teacher ratings of behavior problems, social competence, and peer relationships, self-reports of peer relationships and aggression, maternal reports of parenting and mother–child conflict, academic competence as assessed with standardized tests, and observations of children's disruptive and inattentive behavior at school. Unlike prior studies, we do not use measures of aggressive and violent behavior to assess outcomes because early aggression should predict to a range of negative outcomes of varying levels of severity. Moreover, given the age of our sample, we do not expect to see serious aggression, as assessed by Nagin and colleagues (e.g., Brame et al., 2001; Nagin & Tremblay, 1999), but we do expect to find that children on high stable and high and declining aggression trajectories will evidence peer problems, poor school achievement, and symptoms of externalizing disorders at higher rates than children in the low and moderate/declining groups. Although we expect that children high and low in aggression will differ on most if not all of these indicators of adjustment, we are less certain to what extent children in the declining groups will differ from one another or from the high and low groups.

Chapter VI explores whether a variable-centered approach to studying changes in aggression over time, Hierarchical Linear Modeling (HLM), provides information similar or different from the person-centered approach of trajectory analysis. In a recent *SRCD Monograph*, Hart et al. (2003) examined whether person-centered or variable-centered approaches to the study of personality in early childhood provided more information. They concluded that a person-centered approach was preferable, although to some degree complementary information was obtained from the variable-centered analysis. In Chapter VII, we integrate the findings with prior research, summarize our conclusions, and discuss next steps for work in this area.

II. METHOD AND DATA ANALYSIS

In this chapter, we provide an overview of the NICHD Study of Early Child-Care methods relevant to this report. Methods are organized to parallel the results. First, the measure used to determine trajectories is described followed by baseline and then longitudinal predictors of trajectory membership. This includes measures that were composited using data obtained from 1 to 24 months, predicting membership in trajectory groups and parallel measures obtained after 24 months (36 and 54 months or 36 months through third grade) that were examined as time-varying predictors of trajectory membership. The third set of measures includes third grade outcomes. Finally, several additional measures, used to test specific follow-up hypotheses about particular group contrasts, are described.

PARTICIPANTS

Families were recruited during hospital visits to mothers shortly after the birth of a child in 1991 at ten locations in the U.S. (Little Rock, AR; Irvine, CA; Lawrence, KS; Boston, MA; Philadelphia, PA; Pittsburgh, PA; Charlottesville, VA; Morganton, NC; Seattle, WA; Madison, WI). Recruitment and selection procedures are described in detail in several publications (see NICHD ECCRN, 1997a, b; 2001a; 2002) and our web sites (http://secc.rti.org or www.nichd.nih.gov/crmc/secc). During selected 24-hour intervals, all women giving birth were screened for eligibility and willingness to be contacted again. Of the 8,986 mothers who gave birth during the sampling period, 5,416 (60%) agreed to be telephoned in 2 weeks and met the eligibility requirements (mother over 18, spoke English, mother healthy, baby not multiple birth or released for adoption, live within an hour of research site, move from the area not planned in the next year, neighborhood not deemed too dangerous by police to visit). Of that group, a conditionally random sample of 3,015 was selected (56%) for a 2-week phone call. The conditioning assured adequate representation (at least 10%) of single mothers, mothers without a high school degree, and ethnic minority mothers. At the 2-week call, families were excluded if the baby had been hospitalized for more than 7 days, the family expected to move in the next 3 years, or they could not be reached in at least three attempts at telephone contact. A total of 1,525 families were selected for the call as eligible and agreed to an interview. Of these, 1,364 completed a home interview when the infant was 1 month old and became study participants.

The resulting sample was diverse: 24% were minority, 11% of the mothers had not completed high school, and 14% were single. Mothers had an average of 14.4 years of education. Average family income was 3.6 times the poverty threshold. The participating families were similar to the eligible hospital sample in terms of maternal education, percentage in different ethnic groups, and presence of a husband/partner in the household.

The trajectory analyses conducted for the current report are based on 1,195 children who had at least two out of a possible six mother reports of aggressive behavior between 24 months and third grade (see below). However, given the number of assessments obtained over the course of a nine-year period (from birth to third grade), n's vary because of missing data. These 1,195 children were compared with those not included in this analysis ($n = 169$) on demographic and other indicators at 1 month and on two observational variables assessed at 6 months. Included and excluded children did not differ on child sex (51% and 53% male). However, included children and families were more likely to be white (78% vs. 67%, $p < .01$), and to have a higher income to needs ratio (M's = 3.73 and 2.93, $p = .011$). Mothers included in these analyses had a higher level of education (M's = 14.35 and 13.39, $p < .001$), were more likely to be living with a partner at 1 month (87% vs. 76%, $p < .001$), and reported somewhat lower levels of depressive symptoms at 1 month (M's = 11.18 and 12.68, $p < .05$). Mothers included and excluded from these analyses did not differ on observed maternal sensitivity at 6 months, but those with missing data received lower scores on the HOME observation of the environment at 6 months (M's = 36.69 and 34.97, $p < .01$). Because the NICHD SECC sample excluded children of adolescent mothers, mothers who did not speak English, and children who were hospitalized at birth or who had a diagnosed disability, it is somewhat less inclusive of children experiencing a range of potential risk conditions.

OVERVIEW OF DATA COLLECTION

Children were followed from birth to third grade. Mothers were interviewed in person during home visits when infants were 1 month old.

Detailed measures of home and family environments were obtained via interviews and observations when children were 6, 15, 24, 36, and 54 months old and in first and third grade. Childcare settings were observed from 6 months to 54 months for all children who were in nonmaternal care on a regular basis for 10 or more hours per week. Mothers were telephoned regularly to update reports on childcare usage. These calls occurred every 3 months between 1 and 36 months and every 4 months thereafter until 54 months. Children's cognitive skills and social behavior were assessed at 24, 36, and 54 months and in first and third grades with observational, questionnaire, and test measures obtained during laboratory and home visits. Several additional questionnaire measures were obtained from mothers during the kindergarten year. At third grade children were observed in their classrooms and during lunch for one full day. Teachers also completed questionnaires on study children at third grade. The following sections describe the specific variables used in this monograph and how they functioned in the analyses. Additional details about all data collection procedures, psychometric properties of the instruments, and descriptions of how composites were derived and constructed are documented in Manuals of Operation of the study (http://secc.rti.org/). Readers are referred to these manuals for further information.

MEASURES

Maternal Reports of Aggressive Behavior

At each assessment from 24 months through third grade, mothers completed the Achenbach Child Behavior Checklist (CBCL, Achenbach, 1991a, 1992). The preschool version was completed at 24 and 36 months and the school-age version was completed thereafter (54 months, kindergarten, first grade, third grade). The preschool version includes 99 items and the school-age version includes 113 items that describe typical, but potentially problematic child behaviors. Mothers rated how descriptive each item was of the child's usual behavior over the last 2 months as not true (0), somewhat or sometimes true (1), or very true or often true (2) of the child.

For the current trajectory analyses, six items reflecting overt physical aggression to people, animals, and objects were selected; only items that appeared on both the preschool and school-age versions were selected to maximize comparability over time. These were: (a) destroys own things, (b) destroys others' things, (c) gets in many fights, (d) hits others, (e) physically attacks people, and (f) cruel to animals. Raw scores for the relevant items were summed at each age. Scores could range from 0 to 12. This scale showed adequate internal consistency at each age with coefficient α's ranging from .72 to .77. Descriptive statistics on this measure at the item level and the composite level are presented in detail in Chapter III. Physical aggression items were chosen over more general indices of disruptive behavior to avoid a focus primarily on behaviors that are very common in early childhood (e.g., noncompliance) and because other research suggests that stable physical aggression is a better predictor of risk than other disruptive behaviors (Broidy et al., 2003).

Maternal, Child, and Family Predictors and Correlates of Trajectory Group

Measures of maternal, child, and family characteristics were collected from birth to third grade. In predictive analyses, some measures were composited across the 6-, 15-, and 24-month assessments to obtain a cumulative measure of family context prior to the assessment of children's aggressive behavior. In analyses examining time-varying correlates of trajectory, membership, repeated measures were used, rather than composites.

Demographic Characteristics

During home interviews at 1 month, mothers reported their own *education* (in years) and the study children's race/ethnicity. The presence of a husband/partner in the home was assessed during telephone and in-person interviews at regular intervals between 1 month and third grade. For the predictive analyses, *partner in household* was scored "yes" if a partner was present for half or more of the assessments through 24 months, and "no" if a partner was present either not at all or for fewer than half of the assessments over the first 2 years of the child's life. In the longitudinal analyses, partner presence was scored as "yes" or "no" for each assessment period. For example, if a partner was present at 36 months, but not at 54 months, this was reflected in the longitudinal analyses as a "yes" at 36 months and a "no" at 54 months. Mothers reported family income at 6, 15, 24, 36, and 54 months and at kindergarten, first, and third grade. *Income-to-needs ratios* were calculated from U.S. Census Bureau tables as the ratio of family income to the appropriate poverty threshold for each household size and number of children under 18. In the predictive analyses, these ratios were averaged from 6 to 24 months. In the longitudinal analyses, income-to-needs at each age beyond 24 months was considered a separate variable. A log transformation was applied to the income-to-needs ratio to adjust for its skewed distribution.

29

Maternal depressive symptoms were assessed at 1, 6, 15, 24, 36, and 54 months, first grade and third grade, using the Center for Epidemiological Studies Depression Scale (CES-D; Radloff, 1977), a self-report measure that assesses depressive symptomatology in the general population. It consists of 20 items rated on a 3-point scale, with higher scores reflecting more depressive symptoms. Cronbach α coefficients ranged from .88 to .91. The average of the 1-, 6-, 15-, and 24-month assessments was used in predictive analyses and individual scores across time were used in the longitudinal analyses. Because the scores were quite skewed, a log transformation was used.

Mother–child interactions were videotaped in semi-structured 15-minute observations at 6, 15, 24, 36, and 54 months and at first and third grade. The tasks provided a context for assessing age-appropriate qualities of maternal behavior. The tasks at all ages are described in the Manuals of Operation for the NICHD SECC (http://secc.rti.org/) and involved a free play session at 6 months and developmentally appropriate play and problem-solving tasks at subsequent assessments (15, 24, 36, and 54 months, and first and third grade).

Data were collected across the 10 sites by research assistants who attended centralized training sessions at each age and passed certification tests prior to data collection. In addition, each data collector sent practice videotapes of the data collection procedures to the coding site and these were reviewed before a research assistant was permitted to collect any data.

Mother–child interactions were videotaped and tapes were sent to a central nondata collection site for coding. Coders were blind to other information about the families. At 6, 15, and 24 months, composite *maternal sensitivity* scores were created from the sums of three 4-point ratings (maternal sensitivity to child nondistress, intrusiveness [reversed], and positive regard). The sensitivity composite at 6, 15, and 24 months was averaged to form an index of maternal sensitivity during infancy and toddlerhood. At 36 and 54 months, and at first and third grade, the maternal sensitivity composite was the sum of the three 7-point ratings of supportive presence, respect for autonomy, and hostility (reversed). Cronbach's α's for the sensitivity composites ranged from .70 to .84. Inter-coder reliability was determined by assigning two coders to 19–20% of the tapes randomly drawn at each assessment period. Coders were not aware which tapes were double coded and reliability was assessed throughout the coding period. Inter-coder reliability was calculated as the intra-class correlation coefficient. Reliability coefficients for the composite maternal sensitivity scores used in the current report ranged from .72 to .87.

HOME

The HOME Inventory (Bradley, Mundfrom, Whiteside, Casey, & Barrett, 1994; Caldwell & Bradley, 1984) was used to assess the overall quality of the physical and social resources available to a child in the home. The HOME consists of both direct observation and a semi-structured interview with the mother and has age-appropriate versions for infancy, early childhood, and middle childhood. The focus is on the child as a recipient of stimulation from objects, events, and interactions occurring in the family surroundings. Scores were based on the sum of 45 items, with higher values denoting higher levels of maternal responsiveness, child stimulation, and support to the child. Cronbach's α for the total score was .76 at 6 months and .80 at 15 months. HOME scores from the 6- and 15-month assessments on the Infant/Toddler version were averaged and included in predictive analyses. The Early Childhood version of the HOME was completed at 36 and 54 months (α's of .87 and .82, respectively). At third grade the middle childhood version was administered and the total score (59 items, $\alpha = .82$) was used in the longitudinal analyses.

Prior to data collection in infancy, all observers attended centralized training sessions and were required to maintain reliability by matching a master coder on 90% of items. At later assessments, training was conducted by having home visitors score videotapes coded by the master coder; at each assessment, coders had to match the master coder on at least 90% of items before they were permitted to collect data.

Ideas About Raising Children

The Parental Modernity Scale of Child-Rearing and Educational Beliefs (Shaefer & Edgerton, 1985) is a 30-item, Likert-type questionnaire that was completed by mothers at child age 1 month and again at first grade. This instrument was designed to measure traditional authoritarian and progressive democratic beliefs of parents. The 30 items are scored on a 5-point scale from 1 ("Strongly agree") to 5 ("Strongly disagree"). The scale yields a total score and two subscale scores: Progressive Beliefs (reflects attitudes favoring self-directed child behavior) and Traditional Beliefs (reflects attitudes that child behavior should follow adult directives). The total score was used in the current analyses. Higher scores indicate more *traditional beliefs* about raising children. Internal consistency was .81 at 1 month and .89. at first grade. Test–retest reliability from 1 month to first grade was .77, indicating that childrearing attitudes are remarkably stable.

31

The Bayley Mental Development Index (MDI) is the most widely used measure of cognitive developmental status for children in the first 2 years of life. It assesses sensory perceptual acuity and discriminations; memory, learning, and problem solving; early verbal communication; and the ability to form generalizations and classifications. The extensively revised Bayley (BSID-II; Bayley, 1993) was administered at 24 months. More details are provided in NICHD ECCRN (2000a).

At 36 months, children were administered the Reynell Developmental Language Scale (Reynell, 1991). The scale is composed of 67 items and yields two scores: a verbal comprehension score and an expressive language score. Both scales had adequate internal consistency (.93 and .86, respectively). Because they were highly correlated with one another (.76), a composite of the standard scores was created by averaging them. In addition, the School Readiness subtests from the Bracken Scale of Basic Concepts Scale (Bracken, 1984) were administered at 36 months. These included 61 items assessing color recognition, letter identification, number/counting skills, comparisons, and shape recognition ($\alpha = .93$). The standard score was composited with scores from the Reynell to form an overall measure of *cognitive functioning* at 36 months ($\alpha = .77$).

At 54 months, children's *cognitive functioning* was assessed with subtests from the Woodcock–Johnson Psycho-Educational Battery—Revised (Woodcock & Johnson, 1989, 1990). A composite was computed from standard scores (mean = 100, standard deviation = 15) on five subtests: (a) memory for sentences, (b) incomplete words, (c) picture vocabulary, (d) letter-word identification, and (e) applied problems. These scores were also composited with standard scores on the auditory comprehension and expressive communication scales of the Preschool Language Scale ($\alpha = .87$, Zimmerman, Steiner, & Pond, 1992).

At first grade, cognitive ability and academic achievement were also assessed with five subtests from the Woodcock–Johnson battery: memory for sentences, incomplete words, picture vocabulary, letter-word identification, and applied problems. Standard scores were again computed and averaged to form a composite measure of cognitive functioning.

At each age, examiners at all 10 sites went through rigorous training and certification. They first attended a common training at a central site and then they were required to submit videotapes of test administration. Videotaped administrations were checked against a set of standard criteria that examiners had to meet before they were permitted to collect data.

Child-Care Experiences Prior to School Entry

During telephone interviews conducted at 3-month intervals through 36 months and at 4-month intervals thereafter, mothers reported the types and hours of nonmaternal care that were being used. At 6, 15, 24, 36, and 54 months child-care settings were observed to evaluate child-care quality.

Child-care Quantity

The estimates of quantity of child care were created from maternal telephone reports of hours per week in all nonmaternal care arrangements at regularly scheduled intervals from 1 to 54 months. Hours in care was calculated as the average number of hours per week that the child was in at least 5 hours of nonmaternal care for each epoch (3-month intervals up to 36 months, 4-month intervals between 40 and 54 months). These scores were calculated for data from 1 to 24 months for the predictive analyses. In addition, individual scores were used in longitudinal analyses that included data from 24 months to 54 months. Children who experienced no routine nonmaternal care received scores of zero on these indices. Because the distributions of these variables were quite skewed, a log transformation was applied to the data.

Child-care Quality

Observational assessments of quality were obtained for primary nonmaternal arrangements that were used for 10 or more hours per week at 6, 15, 24, 36, and 54 months. Observations were conducted during two half-day visits scheduled within a 2-week interval at 6–36 months and one half-day visit at 54 months. At each half-day visit, observers completed two 44-minute cycles of the Observational Record of the Caregiving Environment (ORCE, NICHD ECCRN, 1997a, b, 2000b, 2001b) during which they coded the frequency of specific caregiver behaviors and then rated the quality of the caregiving. On average, four ORCE cycles were completed for children from 6 to 36 months and two ORCE cycles were completed at 54 months. ORCE quality ratings were obtained for at least one age period for 985 children and for at least two ages for 779 children.

Positive caregiving composites were calculated at each age. At 6, 15, and 24 months, positive caregiving composite scores were the mean of five 4-point ratings (sensitivity to child's nondistress signals, stimulation of cognitive development, positive regard for child, emotional detachment [reflected], flatness of affect [reflected]). Cronbach's α's for the composite were .89 at 6 months, .88 at 15 months, and .87 at 24 months. At 36 months, these five scales plus two additional subscales, "fosters child's exploration" and "intrusive" [reflected], were included in the composite (Cronbach $\alpha = .83$). At 54 months, the positive caregiving composite was the mean of 4-point ratings of caregivers' sensitivity/responsivity, stimulation of cognitive development, intrusiveness (reflected), and detachment (reflected) (Cronbach $\alpha = .72$).

To ensure that observers at the 10 sites were making comparable ratings, all observers were certified before beginning data collection. The certification test at each age consisted of six 44-minute videotapes that had been master-coded by experts. Exact agreement with the master codes at a level of 60% or better was required. To prevent observer drift, all observers took two additional coding tests during the 10 months of data collection at each assessment age. A criterion of 60% exact agreement was required for continued data collection. In addition, observer agreement was assessed during live on-site observations. At each site, all possible pairs of observers visited both home-based and center-based child care. Inter-observer agreement for the positive caregiving composite scores was computed for the master-coded reliability-test videotapes and for the live observations, using Pearson correlation and the repeated measures ANOVA formulation described in Winer (1971, p. 287). Inter-observer agreement exceeded .90 at 6 months, .86 at 15 months, .81 at 24 months, .80 at 36 months and .90 at 54 months. The average live reliability across all codes, using Winer's method, was .84. For the predictive analyses, an index of *child-care quality* was formed by averaging positive caregiving composite scores for all available time periods in which a particular child's care settings were rated at 6, 15, and 24 months. For the longitudinal analyses, available scores from 24 through 54 months were used.

Type of Child Care

The estimates of time in center care were created from maternal telephone reports obtained regularly of hours per week in all nonmaternal care arrangements from 1 to 54 months. The proportion of epochs that the child spent in at least 10 hours of center care per week was computed for 1–24, 25–36, and 37–54 months. These proportions were highly skewed because very few children attended centers as infants and most children attended centers as preschoolers. For analysis this variable was transformed to a value of 0 if there were no epochs with center care and a value of 1 if the child experienced any center care.

34

Risk Index

In addition, a risk index was calculated at each age based on nine risk factors: (a) poverty, (b) low maternal education, (c) minority ethnic status, (d) single parent, (e) large number of children in the household, (f) maternal depression symptoms, (g) authoritarian child-rearing attitudes, (h) unresponsive maternal interaction style, and (i) low levels of stimulation and responsiveness in the home. Each variable in the index was dichotomized into no risk (0) or risk (1), and the number of items scored 1 was summed. Several of the risk factors were assessed only once (i.e., maternal education, ethnicity, and maternal attitudes), and the other measures were collected longitudinally. Two sets of indices were computed. For 1–24 months, these included: (a) income-to-needs ratio below 2 at the 6-, 15-, or 24-month assessment, (b) no partner in the household at the 6-, 15-, or 24-month assessment, (c) less than a high school education, (d) ethnicity (minority), (e) maternal depressive symptoms at 16 or above at the 6-, 15-, or 24-month assessment, (f) maternal sensitivity in bottom quartile at the 6-, 15-, or 24-month assessment, (g) HOME scores in bottom quartile at 6, 15, or 24 months, (h) traditional ideas about raising children in the top quartile, and (i) more than three children in the household at 6, 15, or 24 months. For the longitudinal analyses, similar scores were calculated at each age based solely on assessments at that age. One measure, the HOME, was not collected at all ages and so we carried forward the previous assessment as an imputation for ages at which the HOME was not collected. This was done because there was high stability in HOME scores over time. Table 1 lists the variables included in the risk index.

Outcome Measures at Third Grade

Teacher Reports of Behavior Problems, Social Competence, and Academic Performance

At third grade teachers completed a number of standard questionnaires describing children's behavior in the classroom, with peers, and with the teacher herself. These included the *Teacher Report Form* (TRF, Achenbach, 1991b), *Disruptive Behavior Disorders Questionnaire* (DBD, Pelham, Gnagy, Greenslade, & Milich, 1992), the *Social Skills Rating System* (SSRS, Gresham & Elliott, 1990), and the *Student–Teacher Relationship Scale* (Pianta, 2001). Teachers also rated the child's academic performance on a 5-point scale from below grade level to above grade level.

Measures of behavior problems were derived from the TRF and DBD. Scores on the two broadband scales of the TRF, *Internalizing Problems* (e.g., too fearful and anxious) and *Externalizing Problems* (e.g., argues a lot), were

TABLE 1

VARIABLES COMPRISING THE RISK INDEX

Variable	Risk Defined as
Income-to-needs	<2.0
Partner in household[a]	No partner
Maternal education[a]	Less than high school
Ethnicity[a]	Minority
Maternal depressive symptoms	16 or above
Maternal sensitivity[a]	Bottom quartile
HOME	Bottom quartile
IDEAS about raising children	Top quartile
Number of children[a]	>3

[a]Risk factor defined in the same way as used in Sameroff's Rochester Study.

utilized in the main analyses. Raw scores were converted into standard *T*-scores, based on normative data for children of the same age. In addition, in completing the DBD teachers rated children on the 26 specific symptoms listed in the DSM-IV (American Psychiatric Association, 1994) to define Attention Deficit Hyperactivity Disorder and Oppositional Defiant Disorder. Symptoms were listed and teachers asked to rate whether the behavior was "not at all" (0), "sometimes" (1), "pretty much" (2), or "very much" (3) a problem for the study child.

Teachers also completed the Student–Teacher Relationship Scale (STRS; Pianta, 2001). The STRS is a widely used assessment of a teacher's view of her relationship with a particular student and accounts for unique variance in the prediction of social and academic outcomes in school-age children. Two composite indices were derived from the STRS and used in the present study as outcome indicators. *Conflict,* assessing the degree of negative interactions and emotions involving the teacher and child, was included as an indicator of problem behavior ($\alpha = .91$). *Closeness*, assessing the degree of warmth, positive emotions, and open communication between child and teacher, was considered an indicator of social competence ($\alpha = .86$).

Social competence was also measured by having teachers complete the school version of the Social Skills Questionnaire from the Social Skills Rating System (SSQ; Gresham & Elliott, 1991). The total score is the sum of all 30 social competence items, with higher scores reflecting higher levels of perceived social competence. The SSQ was normed on a diverse, national sample of children and shows high levels of internal consistency (median = .90) and test–retest reliability (.75–.88). In the current sample, the coefficient α was .94 at third grade.

Finally, teacher reports of *academic functioning* were derived from a rating of current school performance on a 5-point scale (ranging from

1 = below grade level to 5 = excellent). Children rated as performing below grade level were considered to be performing poorly in school.

Maternal Reports of Discipline and Conflict

At the third grade assessment, mothers completed the Raising Children Questionnaire (Greenberger & Goldberg, 1989) that includes 30 statements describing feelings and attitudes about childrearing; statements are rated on a 4-point scale from 1, "definitely no," to 4 "definitely yes." A *harsh control* scale was derived after conducting a principal components analysis of responses in the current sample. It consisted of 9 items ($\alpha = .75$) assessing approval of strict control and use of physical punishment; higher scores reflect maternal reports of harsher discipline.

Mothers also completed the Child–Parent Relationship Scale adapted from the Student–Teacher Relationship Scale (Pianta, 2001). Seven items assessing mother's perception of *conflict* are scored on a 5-point scale (1 = definitely does not apply to 5 = definitely applies). In the current sample, the α coefficient was .84 and higher scores reflect more perceived conflict with the study child.

Cognitive Functioning and Academic Achievement Tests

Children were again administered the Woodcock–Johnson Psychoeducational Battery (Woodcock & Johnson, 1989, 1990) during laboratory visits at third grade. The cognitive composite included standard scores on four subtests: (a) memory for names, (b) memory for sentences, (c) picture vocabulary, and (d) verbal analogies. The achievement score was the composite of five subtests: (a) letter-word identification, (b) passage comprehension, (c) calculation, (d) applied problems, and (e) word attack.

Teacher Reports of Peer Relations

At third grade, teachers also completed a questionnaire designed to measure the child's peer-related behaviors. The questionnaire consists of 43 items derived from several other measures of positive and negative peer behavior, including bullying, exclusion, victimization, and prosocial behavior (Crick, Bigbee, & Howes, 1996; Ladd & Profilet, 1996). Children's behavior with peers was rated on a 3-point scale (0 = not true, 1 = sometimes true, 2 = often true). Principal components analysis of responses in the current sample yielded several internally consistent scales relevant to the current analyses that did not overlap in content with other teacher

37

report measures such as the TRF and SSRS: *asocial* with peers (5 items, $\alpha = .87$), *excluded* by peers (4 items, $\alpha = .91$), *victimized* by peers (7 items, $\alpha = .86$), and uses *relational aggression* with peers (6 items, $\alpha = .87$). In addition, teachers were asked how many classroom friends the study child had (*number of friends*).

Children's Self-Reports of Peer Relations

Children were asked about their relationships with other children during the third grade laboratory visit. Self-reported *loneliness* was assessed with the Loneliness and Social Dissatisfaction Questionnaire (Asher, Hymel, & Renshaw, 1984). The 16 loneliness items were rated on a 5-point scale (1 = not at all true to 5 = always true, $\alpha = .87$), with higher scores reflecting greater feelings of loneliness.

Children also completed the Friendship Quality Questionnaire (Parker & Asher, 1993), a 21-item scale assessing children's views of their relationship with their best friend. Items are rated on a 5-point scale (1 = not at all true to 5 = really true). Twenty items make up the total *friendship quality* score ($\alpha = .87$), with higher scores reflecting more a positive (validation, companionship, disclosure) and less negative (conflict) relationship.

In addition, children's intent attributions in ambiguous situations were assessed with five story stems (Crick, 1995). Children were read five brief stories about a provocative, but ambiguous peer situation, and then they answered questions about the intent of the children in the story. Three of the stories depict acts that could be construed as having hostile intent and being physically aggressive. Two depict a potentially relational provocation. Children were then asked the reasons for the protagonist's behavior and whether the child in the story was trying to be "mean." Forced choice answers were scored so that they reflected either perceived hostile or benign intent. Six items made up the hostile instrumental aggression attribution score ($\alpha = .77$) and four items made up relational aggression attribution score ($\alpha = .62$).

Finally, children completed another questionnaire about their relationships with children at school. It included four items focused on perceived victimization by peers (picked on, kids say mean things, Kochenderfer & Ladd, 1996) and four assessing involvement in bullying (child picks on others, says mean things). Items were rated on a 5-point scale (1 = never to 5 = always). The coefficient α's for the victimization and bullying items were .74 and .77.

Observations of Behavior in School

Children's behavior at school was also observed for an entire day in third grade that included time in the classroom and at lunch. Some behaviors were coded as frequencies in 30-second intervals and others were rated on 7-point scales. Two ratings of disruptive behavior (in the classroom and lunchroom) were considered relevant to these analyses. Because this was a relatively rare event, these were both recoded to binary (yes/no) variables. In addition, a composite of disengaged and off-task behavior (frequencies) observed in the classroom was examined. In terms of social competence, a composite of child involvement in the classroom was constructed from 7-point ratings of children's self-reliance, attention to ongoing classroom activities, and positive relationship with teacher ($\alpha = .78$). Finally, positive engagement with peers at lunch, a composite of 7-point ratings of positive affect and social-cooperative with peers, was included ($\alpha = .83$).

Observers were trained at a central location and they then had to pass a certification test that included scoring videotapes of classroom and lunchroom behavior that had been pre-coded by a panel of master coders. Observers at each site also completed some visits in pairs to establish live inter-observer reliability. Inter-observer agreement (intraclass correlations) for the ratings of disruptive behavior and the codes making up child involvement and social engagement with peers at lunch obtained from the live reliability assessments ranged from .82 to .96. Agreement on the frequencies of disengaged and off-task behavior ranged from .96 to .99.

Descriptive statistics on these outcome variables are presented in Chapter V.

Additional Follow-Up Measures of Impulsivity

Three measures of impulsivity were obtained at 36 and 54 months and are considered as possible explanatory variables in specific follow-up analyses comparing trajectory groups.

At the 36-month assessment, children were observed in a forbidden toy situation. Midway through a 2-hour laboratory visit, the child was shown an attractive toy and allowed to play with it briefly (Ski Boat Crocs). Then the examiner told the child that she had some work to do, that the child could play with other toys (previously played with), but that she/he should not touch the attractive toy until told she could do so. The toy was then placed at arms length from the child and the examiner sat in a corner of the room doing paper work for 2.5 minutes. At the end of the 2.5 minutes, the examiner returned and allowed the child to play with the toy. This procedure was videotaped for later scoring at a central site by individuals unaware of any information about study children. For the purposes of this paper, the variable labeled *active engagement time* was included; it was scored whenever the child manipulated and/or played with the forbidden toy. Inter-rater reliability was .98.

39

At 54 months, children were observed in a standard delay of gratification task. In the middle of a laboratory visit, the child was offered a small immediate reward of candy (m and m's or other preferred food, if the parent objected to candy) or a larger reward later. The child was taught to ring a bell to summon the experimenter who needed to leave the room and then was left to play the "waiting game." The child was given two plates: one with a small amount of food that could be eaten right away (but only after the experimenter was summoned back by a ring of the bell) and another with a larger amount that could only be eaten at the end of the waiting game. Because so many children were able to wait for the entire 7-minute delay interval, this was scored as pass/fail and this dichotomous score was used in the analyses

The Continuous Performance Task (CPT; Rosvold, Mirsky, Sarason, Bransome, & Beck, 1956) was also used to measure impulsivity during the 54-month laboratory visit. Children saw dot-matrix images that were generated by a computer and presented on a 2-inch-square screen. The child was asked to press a button "as fast as you can" each time the target stimulus (i.e., a chair) appeared (44 times) and to inhibit responding to the 176 nontarget stimuli (e.g. butterfly, fish, flower). Stimuli (220) were presented in 22 blocks. The stimulus duration was 500 ms. and the inter-stimulus intervals were 1500 ms. The target stimulus was randomly presented, appearing twice within each block. The test took approximately 7-1/2 minutes. *Impulsivity* was measured by the number of incorrect responses to the nontarget stimuli. The measure of impulsivity derived from the CPT has adequate test–retest reliability in children this age ($r = .65-.74$; Halperin, Sharma, Greenblatt, & Schwartz, 1991). Children's performance on the CPT also has adequate construct validity (Halperin et al., 1991) and predictive validity (e.g., Barkley, 1994; Barkley, Brodzinsky, & DuPaul, 1992; Campbell et al., 1994). Because scores were skewed, a log transformation was applied to this variable.

DATA ANALYSIS

Patterns of Aggressive Behaviors Over Time

Analyses were conducted in three steps. First, maternal reports of aggressive behaviors collected at 24, 36, and 54 months and in kindergarten, first, and third grade were analyzed to describe developmental patterns. Two sets of analyses were conducted. A person-centered trajectory analysis summarized the repeated measures data by identifying prototypic growth curves and by determining which prototypic pattern was most similar to the child's individual growth curve (see Chapter III). A variable-centered analysis was conducted using growth curve modeling. Analyses were conducted using a nonlinear growth curve analysis that allowed for censoring (see Chapter VI). The person-centered analysis resulted in each child being assigned to a trajectory group based on his/her similarity to prototypic growth curves, and the variable-centered analysis resulted in estimated growth curve parameters.

Identification of Characteristics Associated With Developmental Patterns of Aggression

The next set of analyses was designed to identify child, family, and child-care characteristics associated with patterns of change over time in maternal ratings of aggression. Most of these characteristics were collected longitudinally. Two sets of analyses were conducted. The first focused on characteristics measured prior to and concurrent with the mother's first ratings on the CBCL at 24 months. In these analyses, each characteristic was used to predict the aggression growth curve indicators (see first half of Chapters IV and VI), first individually, and then with demographic covariates. The second analysis focused on characteristics assessed at the same times that the CBCL was completed. In these analyses, longitudinal analyses of each characteristic were conducted as a function of aggression growth curve indicators (see second half of Chapters IV and VI). All of these analyses were conducted with and without covariates. The covariates included demographic variables (maternal education, income/needs, ethnicity, maternal partner status) and child gender.

Identification of Child Outcomes at Third Grade Associated With Developmental Patterns of Aggression

The final set of analyses involved examining how child outcomes at third grade differed in relation to aggression growth curve indicators. Children's academic, behavioral, and peer outcomes were analyzed for associations with patterns of change over time in maternal ratings of aggression. The outcomes were grouped by construct, and omnibus tests conducted for each set. Again, analyses were conducted with and without covariates. These are reported in Chapter V and in the last portion of Chapter VI.

III. PERSON-CENTERED TRAJECTORIES OF PHYSICAL AGGRESSION

Recall that mother reports of physically aggressive behavior were collected at ages 24, 36, and 54 months, in kindergarten, and in first and third grade and that six CBCL items were identified as measuring physically aggressive behavior between 2 years and third grade. The items and their frequencies are shown in Table 2. Confirming what we know about the developmental course of aggressive behavior in early childhood, average scores on mother-rated aggression show a steady decline over age. As can be seen in Table 2, at each age, most mothers indicated that their child did not display any of the six problem behaviors, and the proportion of children whose mothers said they ever displayed specific problem behaviors declined over age. For example, 78% of mothers rated their children as "0" on the item "gets in many fights" when they were 2 years old, 89% rated them "0" on this item at age 4.5, and 94% rated their child a "0" on this item by third grade. Five of the six items occurred in 30% or less of the sample at age 2, and declined to less than 15% of children by third grade. The most frequent form of early aggression, hits others, occurred in about 70% of the sample at ages 2 and 3, but declined to 20% by ages 4 and 5 (kindergarten), and to 12% by third grade. Most of the items showed marked declines between 36 and 54 months of age.

The ratings on the six aggression items from the CBCL, each scored 0–2, were summed at each age. The sum was created after demonstrating that as a group the six items showed good internal consistency at each age (α from .72 to .77). Table 3 shows the distribution of the total mother-rated aggression scores, listing the number of children and percent of the sample with each possible score (0–12) at each age. This table makes it clear that the number of children with 0 scores rose from 21% at 24 months to 76% at third grade. Means, standard deviations, and ranges of aggression scores, as well as Cronbach's α' coefficients by age are included in Table 4. The tables illustrate clearly that most children were showing few aggressive behaviors as toddlers and even fewer by third grade. There were, however, a small

TABLE 2

PERCENT OF MOTHERS ENDORSING EACH CBCL ITEM USED TO ASSESS PHYSICAL AGGRESSION

Rating	Destroys Own Things n (%)	Destroys Others' Things n (%)	Gets in Many Fights n (%)	Hits Others/ Cruel, Bully. Mean to Others n (%)	Attacks People n (%)	Cruel to Animals n (%)
24 months						
Never	856 (72%)	855 (72%)	926 (78%)	335 (28%)	986 (84%)	1021(86%)
Sometimes	304 (26%)	304 (26%)	243 (20%)	782 (66%)	183 (15%)	156 (13%)
Often	29 (2%)	29 (2%)	21 (2%)	73 (6%)	14 (1%)	12 (1%)
36 months						
Never	790 (67%)	806 (69%)	914 (78%)	410 (35%)	1017 (87%)	1030 (88%)
Sometimes	354 (30%)	343 (29%)	242 (21%)	712 (61%)	150 (13%)	138 (12%)
Often	32 (3%)	25 (2%)	19 (2%)	53 (5%)	4 (.3%)	8 (1%)
54 months						
Never	831 (79%)	850 (81%)	937 (89%)	833 (79%)	889 (84%)	963 (91%)
Sometimes	207 (20%)	187 (18%)	114 (11%)	214 (20%)	155 (15%)	92 (9%)
Often	18 (2%)	18 (2%)	4 (.4%)	6 (.6%)	9 (1%)	2 (.2%)
Kindergarten						
Never	855 (82%)	840 (80%)	924 (88%)	856 (82%)	965 (93%)	986 (94%)
Sometimes	175 (17%)	189 (18%)	116 (11%)	183 (18%)	71 (7%)	56 (5%)
Often	14 (1%)	15 (1%)	5 (.5%)	7 (.7%)	6 (.6%)	4 (.4%)
Grade 1						
Never	857 (85%)	857 (85%)	925 (92%)	863 (86%)	946 (94%)	969 (96%)
Sometimes	132 (13%)	138 (14%)	75 (7%)	136 (13%)	59 (6%)	38 (4%)
Often	19 (2%)	14 (1%)	8 (.8%)	9 (.9%)	2 (.2%)	2 (.2%)
Grade 3						
Never	878 (87%)	895 (89%)	944 (94%)	863 (87%)	953 (95%)	991 (99%)
Sometimes	120 (12%)	106 (11%)	58 (6%)	120 (12%)	48 (5%)	15 (1%)
Often	6 (.6%)	5 (.5%)	4 (.4%)	1 (.1%)	1 (.1%)	0

Note.—never = 0, sometimes = 1, often = 2.

number of children at each age whose mothers reported a substantial number of aggressive behavior problems. Overall, about one-third of the children (34%) had a score of 0 or 1 at all ages, and only 4% of children ($n = 55$) ever scored above a six. Correlations over time ranged from .29 (24 months to grade 3) to .67 (kindergarten to grade 1), with an average of .50. Not surprisingly, correlations were fairly high between adjacent age points (.58–.67).

A semiparametric, group-based approach as proposed by Nagin (1999) was used to describe children according to their developmental trajectories on the measure of mother-rated physical aggression. This model assumes that the population of children is composed of distinct groups of individuals who show different developmental trajectories. It assumes that individuals within each group are homogeneous in terms of their

TABLE 3
DISTRIBUTION OF AGGRESSION TOTAL SCORES BY AGE

Total Score	0	1	2	3	4	5	6	7	8	9	10	11	12
24 months													
n	253	353	211	151	90	61	33	15	5	5	1	1	1
%	(21%)	(30%)	(18%)	(13%)	(8%)	(5%)	(3%)	(1%)	(.4%)	(.4%)	(.1%)	(.1%)	(.1%)
36 months													
n	293	324	189	158	85	62	32	17	3	2	1	0	1
%	(25%)	(28%)	(16%)	(14%)	(7%)	(5%)	(3%)	(1%)	(.3%)	(.2%)	(.1%)		(.1%)
54 months													
n	596	179	118	64	38	28	17	6	2	1	1	0	0
%	(57%)	(17%)	(11%)	(6%)	(4%)	(3%)	(2%)	(1%)	(.2%)	(.1%)	(.1%)		
Kindergarten													
n	645	165	103	59	38	17	11	0	2	0	1	1	0
%	(62%)	(16%)	(10%)	(6%)	(4%)	(2%)	(1%)		(.2%)		(.1%)	(.1%)	
Grade 1													
n	715	121	73	47	24	12	6	4	5	2	0	0	0
%	(71%)	(12%)	(7%)	(5%)	(2%)	(1%)	(.6%)	(.4%)	(.5%)	(.2%)			
Grade 3													
n	760	110	61	38	15	17	4	0	1	0	0	0	0
%	(76%)	(11%)	(6%)	(4%)	(1%)	(2%)	(.4%)		(.1%)				

Note.—Maximum possible score = 12.

developmental patterns, and in this respect it is similar to diagnostic classifications or cluster group membership. That is, as with diagnostic categories or clusters, all individuals within a group are viewed analytically as equivalent, based on the belief that within group differences are much less informative than between-group differences.

This analytic approach involves estimating individual growth curves for each child, and then identifying prototypic group curves from these individual curves (Nagin, 1999). The group curves are selected to represent different developmental patterns in a way that optimally describes the data. The degree to which each individual's growth curve resembles each of the prototypic group curves is estimated, and individuals are typically classified into clusters or trajectories accordingly. Each analysis is based on a specified type of growth curve (e.g., linear, quadratic), the number of groups or clusters, and the distribution of the outcome measure over time. Recommended practice involves fitting a series of analyses specifying different numbers of groups and selecting the solution that accounts for the most information in the data as indicated by the Bayesian Information Criterion (BIC).

This approach offers several advantages over standard longitudinal analysis. First, it uses the data to determine the optimal number of groups needed to describe different patterns of change over time (i.e., developmental trajectories). Second, it avoids having to make strong assumptions

TABLE 4

MEANS, STANDARD DEVIATIONS (SD), RANGES, AND INTERNAL RELIABILITIES OF AGGRESSION
SCORES BY AGE

	N	α	Mean	SD	Min.	Max.
24 months	1156	.72	1.96	1.83	0	12
36 months	1158	.72	1.88	1.81	0	12
54 months	1044	.75	1.03	1.59	0	10
Kindergarten	1037	.73	0.85	1.43	0	11
Grade 1	1002	.77	0.68	1.39	0	9
Grade 3	978	.74	0.50	1.11	0	8

Note.—Maximum possible score = 12.

about the population distribution of the developmental trajectories. It is rare that there is sufficient knowledge about the shape, level, and patterns of change in developmental outcomes within the population to specify trajectories a priori; thus, the semiparametric, group-based approach offers a means to estimate this from the data (Burchinal & Appelbaum, 1991).

There are also several disadvantages. First, as a group-based analysis, it makes the debatable assumption that all individuals within the same cluster or trajectory show exactly the same pattern of change over time. Thus, the information in the continuous longitudinal data is reduced to group membership. When the groups are qualitatively different, however, this reduction in information can result in greater precision in analyses that aim to identify either antecedents or outcomes related to developmental patterns. If the groups show only quantitatively different patterns, then it is likely that this approach reduces the power to detect the factors associated with the developmental trajectories (Burchinal & Appelbaum, 1991; Hart et al., 2003). Second, it is often more difficult to conduct subsequent analyses, and especially to account for Type I errors, because the developmental trajectories are represented by categorical variables. Analyses designed to identify predictors of developmental patterns must involve either logistic or multinomial analyses in which the outcomes are categorical or require the examination of predictors individually.

With these caveats in mind, the semiparametric, group-based trajectory analysis was performed using the maternal ratings of aggression on all children who had at least two of the possible six measurements over the study period (i.e., 24, 36, and 54 months, kindergarten, grade 1, grade 3; $N = 1195$). A zero-inflated Poisson distribution was indicated because the distribution of these scores was highly skewed and could be viewed as a count variable, i.e., a count of the number of aggressive problem behaviors, weighted by frequency of occurrence. A cubic growth curve model was specified to describe the pattern of change over time. As recommended by

TABLE 5

BAYESIAN INFORMATION CRITERION (BIC) BY NUMBER OF GROUPS*

Model	BIC Score
Group 2	− 8948
Group 3	− 8171
Group 4	− 8079
Group 5	− 8040
Group 6	− 8034
Group 7	− 8044
Group 8	− 8089

*A larger BIC indicates a better model fit.

Nagin (1999), we examined the Bayesian Information Criterion and the trajectories to decide on the model that best fit the data. Using the BIC score, a five-group model was clearly better than a four-group model (Table 5), because the BIC score for the five-group model was larger. However, there was only a small difference between the BIC for the five- and six-group models. Upon examining the trajectories it was decided to err on the side of parsimony and to use the five-group model to retain power for follow-up analyses, as the six-group model identified three low groups (instead of the two described below) of limited theoretical interest. The observed trajectories as described by the five-group model are depicted in Figure 1.

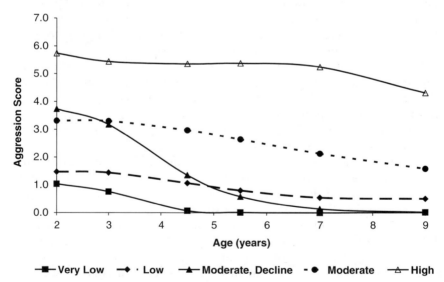

FIGURE 1.—Observed trajectories of mother-rated aggression.

TABLE 6

MEANS (M) AND STANDARD DEVIATIONS (SD) OF AGGRESSION TOTAL SCORES AT EACH AGE BY
TRAJECTORY GROUP

	Age					
Trajectory	24 months M (SD)	36 months M (SD)	54 months M (SD)	Kindergarten M (SD)	First Grade M (SD)	Third Grade M (SD)
Very low	1.06 (1.06)	0.79 (0.89)	0.07 (0.25)	0.00 (0.07)	0.00 (0.00)	0.02 (0.13)
Low	1.36 (0.99)	1.59 (1.10)	1.02 (1.11)	0.88 (0.89)	0.64 (0.86)	0.54 (0.85)
Moderate declining	4.33 (1.84)	3.50 (1.50)	1.39 (1.34)	0.63 (0.78)	0.10 (0.30)	0.01 (0.09)
Moderate	3.26 (1.59)	3.70 (1.67)	2.81 (1.70)	2.77 (1.37)	2.30 (1.37)	1.57 (1.36)
High	5.69 (2.45)	6.03 (2.06)	5.34 (2.07)	5.12 (2.36)	5.92 (1.90)	4.50 (1.44)

Note.—*N*'s for group are based on children with at least two maternal ratings of aggression: group 1(n =
547); group 2 *(n = 302)*; group 3 *(n = 132)*; group 4 *(n = 184)*; group 5 *(n = 30)*.

Model fit is also indexed by a probability score that is calculated to indicate how well each child fits the assigned trajectory. The mean probability
scores for trajectory groups ranged from .76 to .90, with children in the two
most extreme groups [i.e., consistently low (.88) or consistently high (.90), see
below] having the highest overall probability of correct classification. Overall,
the model fit was good to excellent according to this criterion.

Descriptive statistics on aggression scores by age and trajectory group
are summarized in Table 6. These trajectory groups show interesting differences in both mean level of aggression as rated by mothers and rates of
change over time in aggression scores from 24 months to third grade. As
Figure 1 illustrates, the first two trajectories show low overall levels of aggression. Group 1 is a *very low-aggression* trajectory group with a mean score
of only 1 (out of a possible 12) at 24 months and a rapid decline to almost 0
by 54 months. Almost half the sample (45%) is in this low-aggression trajectory group, with a mean probability coefficient of .88. Another 25% of
the study children are clustered in trajectory 2 (*low aggression*), which is quite
low in aggression throughout, albeit slightly higher than group 1 (mean
probability = .79). These children likewise show a decline in aggression, but
they do not reach a score of 0. Overall, however, 70% of the sample is in
these two low-to-no aggression trajectory groups. Clearly, according to
mothers' reports, most children are not especially aggressive, although at 24
months some aggressive behavior seems to be normative.

One trajectory group shows a marked decline in aggressive behavior
over time. Group 3, 12% of the sample, is initially rated as moderate in
aggression, with mean scores of 4.3 at 24 months, but with a steep decline at
54 months and then a further decline to about 0 by first grade. These

developmental changes in aggression suggest that this group might be showing age-related and transient aggressive behavior related to emerging autonomy and limit-testing. This group shows a *moderate and steeply declining* aggression trajectory (mean probability = .76).

The final two groups show moderate to high and relatively stable levels of aggression. Group 4, 15% of the sample, is moderate in aggression at 24 and 36 months; despite a downward trajectory over time through third grade, however, this group remains elevated relative to groups 1–3 and appears to be on a *moderately stable*, albeit *slightly declining* aggression trajectory (mean probability = .85). The slight discrepancies between the numbers in Table 6 and in Figure 1 reflect the fact that Table 6 is based on unweighted mean scores on the aggression measure for all children assigned to that trajectory group, whereas Figure 1 was generated by the trajectories program and is calculated as the weighted mean of all individuals in the sample using the likelihood of being in each trajectory group as the weight.

Finally, consistent with prior research across the age range (e.g., Broidy et al., 2003; Shaw et al., 2003), 3% of the sample falls into a *high-aggression* trajectory group (mean probability = .90). Although there is a slight decrease in aggression from 36 months to kindergarten in this group, there is also a slight increase in first grade (age 7), and then a slight decrease again at third grade (age 9). Taken together, however, this group is markedly higher than the other four groups at each and every assessment.

SUMMARY AND NEXT STEPS

In summary, approximately 82% of the sample was assigned to trajectories characterized by low to moderate levels of mother-rated aggression at 24 months (groups 1–3); even when these children show some aggression early on, they decline to very low levels by third grade. However, children in two trajectories comprising the remaining 18% of the sample are consistently higher throughout the study period. Group 4 is moderately high, with some decline at grade 3. Group 5, the smallest group, is consistently very high relative to other groups, despite small increases and decreases over the course of development. It is also noteworthy that consistent with prior reports, there is no group that shows an increase in aggression with age (Nagin & Tremblay, 1999; Tremblay, 2000). Even the highest group is not rated as more aggressive in third grade than they were at earlier ages, especially at 36 months.

Of particular interest in the following chapters will be the early predictors, time-varying correlates, and outcomes of trajectory membership. In addition, specific contrasts are of interest. First, if we consider groups 1 and

2 as consistently low and group 3 as showing age-related, but transient aggression, it is important to explore whether early family stress, child characteristics, or child care experiences are associated with the temporary and moderately elevated level of aggression in group 3, and also whether there are any sequelae of this early aggressive behavior in third grade. Thus, we will examine planned contrasts between the two low-aggression trajectory groups (1 and 2) and group 3 (moderate and steeply declining aggression) in subsequent chapters. In addition, if we consider groups 1 and 2 as the normative groups, it is important to compare them with the two higher aggression groups to answer the question of what differentiates those on low-aggression trajectories from those on consistently higher trajectories of aggression. Thus, planned contrasts between the two low trajectory groups (1, 2) and the moderate group (4) and between the two low groups and the consistently high group (5) will be examined.

Comparison of the moderate and steeply declining group (3) and the moderate and stable group (4) is also of interest. It is noteworthy that their trajectory lines cross at 36 months and continue to diverge more and more over the course of development. Thus, it is important to examine early and continuing contrasts between these two groups, not only on risk indicators and third grade outcomes, but on other measures that reflect self-regulation and impulse control at 36 and 54 months.

Finally, planned contrasts between the moderate group (4) and the high and stable group (5) are important. Are these groups merely showing differences in the magnitude of their aggression over time or does it appear that the aggression of the children in the stable and high group is more intense and hostile than the aggression of the children in the moderate group? Follow-up analyses will address these questions.

IV. PREDICTORS OF AGGRESSION TRAJECTORIES

In this chapter we report the child, family, and child-care factors that are associated with trajectory group membership. First, we sought to identify antecedents that predicted membership in the five developmental aggression trajectories described in Chapter III. We asked whether membership in the five trajectory groups was predicted by measures of demographic, family, child, and child-care characteristics that preceded or were collected at the same time as the mother's first aggression rating to identify early factors that discriminated among the aggression trajectory groups. Second, we asked whether change over time on demographic, child, family, and child-care characteristics that were collected concurrently with the maternal ratings accounted for differences among the trajectory groups. That is, we wanted to know how the groups differed prior to the first maternal rating of aggressive behavior and how they differed over time during the same period that the mothers completed their ratings of the child's aggressive behavior.

First, the five trajectory groups were compared on selected demographic, child, family, and child-care characteristics. These included four demographic characteristics: family income, maternal education, presence of a partner in the household, and child ethnicity. We anticipated that membership in trajectories characterized by higher levels of aggression (groups 4 and 5) would be predicted by lower income and maternal education, and lower levels of partner presence. We also expected that children in the trajectory group that showed a steep decline in the level of aggressive behavior (group 3) would be more likely to experience a decrease in family risk. For example, a father-figure might enter the household or family income might increase over time, concomitant with the decrease in mother-ratings of aggression. Of these demographic characteristics, two were collected longitudinally (income and partner in the household) and two were considered time-invariant (maternal education and ethnicity).

We selected two child characteristics, gender and cognitive developmental level, because we believed that trajectory groups characterized by higher levels of aggression would be more likely to be male and to be functioning at a lower cognitive level. Gender, of course, was a time-invariant predictor, but cognitive level was collected longitudinally. Stable and high levels of aggression were especially likely to be associated with being a boy and with low, and possibly declining levels of cognitive functioning.

We had similar expectations regarding trajectory group differences on the four family and three child-care characteristics selected for examination. The family variables included the observations of maternal sensitivity and the family environment, maternal childrearing attitudes, and maternal ratings of depressive symptoms. We expected that children in the low-aggression trajectory groups, in contrast to those on the moderate or high-aggression trajectories, would live in more supportive families characterized by higher levels of responsive, sensitive, and child-centered parenting and lower levels of maternal depressive symptoms. The child-care variables included the amount of child care (average hours per week), ratings of child-care quality, and whether the child experienced center care. We also expected that children with higher levels of aggression would experience longer hours of less sensitive child care. Finally, we examined the proportion of time in center care, because the large peer group experience associated with center care may be related to early levels of aggression (NICHD ECCRN, 2003a).

Based on the aggression trajectories identified in Chapter III, five a priori contrasts were examined in each of the antecedent and time-varying analyses discussed above. These contrasts sought to answer four questions related to levels of aggression and to changes in the level of aggression over time:

(1) What distinguishes children who exhibit moderate or high levels of relatively stable aggression from those who follow consistently low-aggression trajectories?

(2) A parallel question also concerns differences between higher and relatively lower levels of aggression: what distinguishes children who exhibit the highest level of aggression over time from those with a more moderate, slightly declining level of mother-reported aggression?

(3) What distinguishes children who exhibit moderately elevated aggression at 24 months that then declines steeply from those with low initial levels at 24 months, given that the groups then converge to show similarly low levels of mother-rated aggression by school entry? Recall that one group shows a sharp decline from moderate to very low levels of aggressive behavior

51

by third grade, whereas the two low groups show consistently low levels of aggression over time. Thus, these groups start out looking different in their levels of aggression at 24 months, but end up at the same point by 54 months.

(4) Conversely, what distinguishes children who exhibit moderate and only slightly declining aggression from those with similarly elevated aggression at 24 months that then declines sharply to a low level by 54 months? Importantly, these groups look similar in level of mother-rated aggression in early childhood, but the curves diverge sharply by 54 months and continue to do so through third grade.

To explore the differences between the two groups showing moderate, but diverging patterns of aggressive behavior between 36 and 54 months further, we analyzed the risk index score and examined changes in this variable from 24 to 54 months because we had predicted that decreases in aggression would be associated with corresponding decreases in family risk. The risk index for 24 months was calculated as 1 point for each risk factor that was present at any time between 1 and 24 months (see Table 1). The longitudinal indices were calculated based on measures collected at that assessment age for measures collected longitudinally. When measures were not collected between these time points the baseline measures were carried forward (e.g., the HOME was not collected at 24 months, and so the 15-month assessment was used to compute 24-month risk). The measures that were collected over time were: income-to-needs, partner in household, maternal depressive symptoms, observed maternal sensitivity, HOME, and number of children in the household. Number of children was included to parallel the risk indices used by Rutter (1979) and Sameroff et al. (1993).

ANTECEDENTS OF PHYSICAL AGGRESSION TRAJECTORIES

The first set of analyses included demographic, child, family, and child-care characteristics from the study child's first 2 years of life to predict trajectory group from variables assessed prior to and concurrent with the age at which mothers first rated their children's aggression. For these analyses, we computed the mean across time for the 1–24 or 6–24 month longitudinal measures. For example, the average income-to-needs ratio was computed from the 6-, 15-, and 24-month interviews to represent the "antecedent" income. Descriptive statistics by trajectory group are presented in Table 7 and the test statistics and effects sizes are given in Table 8. The n's in Table 7 differ slightly from those reported in Chapter III because of missing data.

TABLE 7

MEANS AND STANDARD DEVIATIONS (SD) FOR EARLY PREDICTORS OF MEMBERSHIP IN THE FIVE TRAJECTORY GROUPS

N	Group 1 Very Low 543		Group 2 Low 301		Group 3 Moderate/Decline 130		Group 4 Moderate 182		Group 5 High 29	
	Mean	SD	Mean	SD	Mean	SD	Mean	SD	Mean	SD
Sociodemographics										
Income/needs (mean 6–24 months)	4.10	3.05	3.53	2.79	3.70	2.99	3.00	2.11	2.10	2.70
Log (income/needs)[a]	1.16	.75	.98	.81	1.00	.85	.82	.86	.28	.94
Maternal education, 1 month	14.74	2.44	14.35	2.45	14.35	2.45	13.71	2.18	12.38	1.76
Partner in household (>50% time 1–24 months)	91%		88%		86%		84%		79%	
Race: majority, 1 month	80%		79%		73%		76%		55%	
Child characteristics										
Male (y/n)	46%		50%		57%		60%		72%	
Child cognition (24 months)	94.13	14.21	92.43	14.22	90.14	14.20	89.42	15.51	81.22	13.73
Family/maternal characteristics										
Maternal sensitivity (mean 6–24 months)	9.50	1.22	9.37	1.40	9.18	1.33	9.03	1.38	8.33	1.34
HOME environment (mean 6–15 months)	37.64	3.69	37.18	3.83	36.23	4.27	36.00	5.21	32.72	4.63
Traditional ideas for raising children, 1 month	57.69	14.70	60.61	14.59	58.96	15.89	62.65	14.57	72.72	13.53
Maternal depressive symptoms (mean 1–24 months)	7.89	5.77	9.61	6.31	11.27	7.50	12.47	7.00	18.00	7.81
Log maternal depressive symptoms[a] 1–24 months)	1.98	.66	2.18	.63	2.32	.65	2.46	.58	2.85	.47
Child care										
Child-care quality (mean 6–24 months)	2.95	0.50	2.88	0.48	2.89	0.43	2.85	0.47	2.57	0.59
Proportion in center care (1–24 months)	.11	.23	.12	.25	.08	.19	.09	.21	.05	.15
Any center care[a]	25%		28%		23%		22%		21%	
Total hours/week care (1–24 months)	20.53	14.34	21.61	14.66	16.95	14.85	19.12	14.45	15.84	13.48
Log hours/week[a]	2.64	1.15	2.89	1.17	2.61	1.34	2.82	1.22	2.80	1.11
Risk index										
Cumulative risk at 24 months	2.13	1.93	2.52	2.05	2.98	2.40	2.98	2.17	5.14	2.34

[a]Transformed variable used in analysis due to skewed distribution.

53

TABLE 8

FAMILY, CHILD, AND CHILD-CARE CHARACTERISTICS IN THE CHILD'S FIRST 2 YEARS AS PREDICTORS OF TRAJECTORY GROUP

Predictor	Model Without Covariates						Model With Covariates[a,b]					
	Group χ^2	3 vs. 1,2 Effect Size	4 vs. 1,2 Effect Size	5 vs. 1,2 Effect Size	4 vs. 3 Effect Size	5 vs. 4 Effect Size	Group χ^2	3 vs. 1,2 Effect Size	4 vs. 1,2 Effect Size	5 vs. 1,2 Effect Size	4 vs. 3 Effect Size	5 vs. 4 Effect Size
Demographics												
Income	47.9***	.88	.72***	.44***	.80	.49***	13.1*	.88	.72	.30*	.44	.49*
Maternal education	42.5***	.87	.69***	.37***	.79*	.43**	10.4*	.87	.69*	.37*	.79	.43
Race: Majority	12.1*	.68	.84	.31**	1.21	.45	4.4					
Partner in household (y/n)	9.3						2.4					
Child characteristics												
Child cognition (24 months)	31.4***	.79*	.76***	.45***	.96	.57**	3.7					
Male (y/n)	17.9***	1.45*	1.68**	2.89*	1.16	1.96	16.8**	1.45*	1.68**	2.89*	1.16	1.96
Parenting												
Maternal depression (6–24 months)	102***	1.54***	2.02***	5.26***	1.31*	3.44***	73.3***	1.54***	2.02***	5.26***	1.31	3.44**
Mat sensitivity (6–24 months)	33.3***	.81*	.74***	.47***	.92	.58**	3.5					
HOME environment (6–15 months)	46.9***	.73***	.71***	.47***	.97	.64**	13.6**	.73**	.70*	.47**	.97	.64
Traditional Ideas for raising children (1 month)	36.0***	.98	1.26***	2.70***	1.28*	2.76**	8.6					
Risk index[b]	64.8***	1.40***	1.40***	3.23***	1.0	2.30*						
Child care[c]												
Total hours/week (1–24 months)	11.2*	.76**	.90	.80	1.18	.94	5.1					
Center care (6–24 months)	3.3						1.7					
Child-care quality (6–24 months)	11.6**	.93	.87	.52*	.93	.56*	5.1					

Note.—Groups 1 and 2 are low in aggression; group 3 is moderate in aggression and declines steeply; group 4 is moderate in aggression and declines slightly; group 5 is high in aggression. Effect sizes are reported as the increase (if greater than 1)/decrease (if less than 1) in the odds ratio.

[a] Covariates in second model include ethnicity (white/not), gender, maternal education, partner in household and natural log of income/needs ratio. The only covariate included in analysis of risk index is gender because index created from these covariates.

[b] Risk index was not examined with covariates because they were used as risk variables in computing the risk index.

[c] Child-care hours, type, and quality also added to second model when child care variables were examined.

*$p < .05$.
**$p < .01$.
***$p < .001$.

Multinomial regression analyses were used to predict trajectory group membership from selected family, child, and child-care characteristics. Analyses were conducted twice, once without covariates and once including covariates: gender, maternal education, family income (log of income/ needs), whether the mother had a partner in the household, and child ethnicity. In Table 8 each row presents results from a separate analysis, that is, a single predictor (on the left) or a single predictor adjusted for the five covariates (on the right). When group differences were detected, the effect sizes for the a priori specified contrasts were calculated. The effect sizes were computed as odds ratios. An odds ratio reflects the extent to which a predictor differentially increases the probability of being in one group over the other. For categorical predictors, the effect size was $d = \text{Exp}(B)$, the odds ratio for that categorical variable. For example, an odds ratio of 2.89 for gender in comparing group 5 with groups 1 and 2 means that the odds of being a male in group 5 were 2.89 times higher than the odds of being male in groups 1 and 2 (see Table 8). Similarly, an odds ratio of .31 for ethnicity in the comparison of group 5 with groups 1 and 2 means that the odds of being white in group 5 were about one-third the odds of being white in groups 1 and 2. For continuous predictors effect sizes were computed as: $d = \text{Exp}(B + \sigma_X)$. They should be interpreted as the odds ratio associated with a 1 SD unit change in the predictor.

Multinomial regression analyses predicting trajectory group membership were conducted first without covariates. Follow-up comparisons were conducted when overall group differences were indicated. Results are shown on the left side of Table 8 under the heading "Model without Covariates." As the table indicates, the five trajectory groups differ on all selected 1–24-month characteristics except for presence of a partner in the household and whether the child experienced center care.

In general, when covariates were not controlled, income, maternal education, early parenting variables (maternal sensitivity, HOME, attitudes toward childrearing, depressive symptoms), and child gender and cognition predicted membership in trajectory groups. Less positive parenting, being a boy, and lower cognitive functioning were associated with membership in one of the moderate- to high-aggression trajectories. The moderate-aggression group and the high-aggression group also differed from each other on all these measures except child gender. As can be seen in Table 7, the two lowest aggression groups were split fairly evenly between boys and girls (46–50%), whereas the high and stable group was 72% male; given the small n for this high and stable group, it included only eight girls. Hours in child care also predicted trajectory group membership, with contrasts indicating that children in the moderate, but steeply declining aggression group were in fewer hours of child care from early infancy through 24 months than those consistently lowest in aggression. On the other hand, the

55

group on the highest aggression trajectory was in lower quality child care in infancy than those children who were low or moderate in aggression.

Because membership in the high- and moderate-aggression trajectories was predicted by most risk indicators, it is then not surprising that the overall risk index also predicted trajectory membership. The means in Table 7 indicate a relatively linear relationship between the level of the risk index and level of aggression. However, children in the high-risk group experienced considerably more risk than children in the other four groups, whereas the two low-aggression groups differed from those showing even modest and declining aggression. The odds ratios quantify these differences between children in the highest aggression trajectory group and the low-aggression groups (OR = 3.23) and the moderate and only slightly declining group (OR = 2.30). The two groups with modest early aggression, but different developmental trajectories (i.e., steeply declining vs. slightly declining) did not differ in initial levels of family risk, which was modest, but still somewhat higher than the level of risk in the two low-aggression groups (OR = 1.40).

The second set of analyses identified which early demographic, child, family, and child-care characteristics distinguished among the five trajectory groups after adjusting for the demographic characteristics included as covariates. In these analyses, trajectory group membership was predicted from early child, family, and child-care characteristics after adjusting for ethnicity, gender, maternal education, partner in household, and income/ needs. The risk indices were not examined in these analyses because the demographic covariates were included. Results are shown on the right side of Table 8. When all the covariates were considered together, income and maternal education continued to predict trajectory group membership uniquely, and in general, children in the more aggressive trajectory groups came from families with lower incomes and less maternal education. With family demographic covariates controlled, membership in the trajectory groups continued to be predicted by early symptoms of maternal depression, the HOME, and being a boy. Children either moderate or high in aggression were more likely to be boys (OR from 1.45 to 2.89) whose mothers reported higher levels of depressive symptoms (OR from 1.54 to 5.26) and provided them with a less stimulating environment (OR from .47 to .73) than did mothers of children on the two low-aggression trajectories. As with overall risk, the two moderate-aggression trajectory groups (steeply and slightly declining) did not differ from one another on these early predictors, but the mothers of children high in aggression reported more depressive symptoms than did mothers of children in the moderate, slightly declining trajectory group (OR = 3.44). With covariates controlled, the few differences on child-care measures became nonsignificant.

CONCURRENT PATTERNS OF CHANGE IN PREDICTORS OF AGGRESSION TRAJECTORIES

The next set of analyses was designed to identify time-varying demographic, family, child care, and child characteristics that might account for differences in patterns of change in the trajectory groups. These included income to needs ratio, presence of a partner in the household, maternal depressive symptoms, maternal sensitivity, stimulation in the family environment (HOME), and children's cognitive functioning assessed through third grade, and quality, quantity (number of hours), and type of child care (center care or not) assessed through 54 months. Tables 9 and 10 provide descriptive statistics for the family, child, and child-care characteristics examined in these repeated measures analyses by aggression trajectory.

Longitudinal analyses were conducted using hierarchical linear models (Bryk & Raudenbush, 2002) for continuous outcomes and logistic regression based on a generalized estimating equation approach (Liang & Zeger, 1986) for categorical outcomes. The model in both cases included as predictors: gender, month, $month^2$, group, month × group, and $month^2$ group. The analysis estimated the main effect for group at the age of 24 months by centering age at 24 months. For these repeated measures analyses, we estimated the difference in effect on the characteristics of interest according to the pre-specified group contrasts presented earlier.

Results from the analyses are presented on the left side of Table 11. The first column under the heading "model without covariates" lists the F or χ^2 statistic for the five-group comparison. The next five columns list the t or χ^2 statistic for the specified contrasts. Effect sizes for the individual contrasts were reported only if the test of omnibus group differences was significant at the $\alpha = 0.05$ level. Group differences at baseline are reported on the first row under each outcome variable labeled "group main effect." Differences in the 24-month third-grade trajectories over time are reported on the second row under each outcome variable reflecting differential change as a function of trajectory group, labeled "Group × age." Effect sizes for these analyses were computed as the standardized difference between adjusted group means:

$$D = \text{adjusted}\,M_1 - \text{adjusted}\,M_2/\sigma_Y.$$

These analyses indicated that the five trajectory groups differed on most of the selected characteristics examined longitudinally: income, whether a partner was present in the household, maternal sensitivity, stimulation in home environment, maternal depressive symptoms, cognitive functioning, number of hours in child care, and cumulative social risk, consistent with the analyses already reported. However, changes over time on the selected

57

TABLE 9

MEANS AND STANDARD DEVIATIONS (SD) OF FAMILY, CHILD, AND CHILD-CARE CHARACTERISTICS FROM 24 MONTHS TO 3RD GRADE BY TRAJECTORY

| | Aggression Trajectory Group | | | | | | | | | | | | | | |
| | 1 | | | 2 | | | 3 | | | 4 | | | 5 | | |
	N	Mean	SD	N	Mean	SD	N	Mean	SD	N	Mean	SD	N	Mean	SD
Demographics															
Partner in household (proportion)															
24 months	535	.88		294	.88		130	.82		178	.81		29	.62	
36 months	539	.86		301	.85		129	.81		178	.77		29	.66	
54 months	482	.87		279	.86		121	.78		160	.78		28	.64	
Kindergarten	471	.86		275	.83		120	.80		155	.78		27	.63	
Grade 1	460	.85		263	.83		119	.76		157	.76		26	.63	
Grade 3	466	.88		270	.81		120	.75		156	.76		28	.64	
Income/needs															
24 months	534	4.09	2.99	287	3.68	2.90	126	3.59	2.61	173	2.90	1.87	29	2.07	2.58
36 months	538	4.02	3.02	297	3.46	2.74	127	3.59	2.88	177	2.70	1.90	29	2.10	2.46
54 months	480	3.96	2.72	274	3.37	2.53	120	3.70	2.99	157	2.77	1.94	28	1.87	2.26
Kindergarten	458	3.90	2.66	267	3.27	2.51	115	3.78	3.22	156	2.69	1.97	24	1.76	1.60
Grade 1	440	4.41	2.92	250	3.74	2.94	113	4.16	3.32	149	3.00	2.14	25	2.04	1.93
Grade 3	426	4.89	3.36	249	3.89	2.99	107	4.46	3.57	145	3.28	2.36	25	2.08	1.94
Family characteristics															
Maternal depression															
24 months	499	7.42	7.23	275	9.18	8.19	117	10.18	8.74	168	12.97	9.26	28	20.21	12.3
36 months	533	7.02	6.67	300	9.56	8.28	129	10.97	10.30	176	12.53	8.73	28	15.79	9.62
54 months	477	7.86	7.87	277	9.12	8.23	121	10.12	9.08	160	13.38	9.29	28	17.04	8.28
Grade 1	449	6.45	7.52	257	8.58	8.26	117	9.19	8.57	154	12.00	9.68	25	13.80	7.69
Grade 3	443	6.90	7.17	257	9.49	8.98	114	9.56	8.71	153	12.67	10.50	26	15.97	9.01

Table 9. (Contd.)

	Aggression Trajectory Group														
	1			2			3			4			5		
	N	Mean	SD	N	Mean	SD	N	Mean	SD	N	Mean	SD	N	Mean	SD
Maternal sensitivity															
24 months	521	9.58	1.58	287	9.44	1.80	129	9.24	1.82	176	8.97	1.83	27	8.33	1.82
36 months	519	10.09	1.31	289	9.91	1.49	125	10.00	1.47	176	9.33	1.70	28	7.61	2.19
54 months	467	9.94	1.48	267	9.79	1.58	113	9.44	1.86	155	9.31	1.66	27	8.57	1.93
Grade 1	445	9.90	1.57	256	9.69	1.76	116	9.57	1.61	154	9.22	1.81	25	8.27	1.99
Grade 3	426	9.65	1.28	246	9.37	1.33	108	9.37	1.42	149	8.61	1.53	24	8.38	1.91
HOME total															
15 months	535	.19	.88	296	.02	.89	129	−.17	.99	177	−.21	.96	29	−1.07	1.14
36 months	528	.20	.89	289	−.01	.98	126	−.06	.91	174	−.28	1.06	28	−1.40	1.11
54 months	470	.27	.81	265	.00	.91	116	−.04	.96	154	−.45	1.03	28	−1.53	1.09
Grade 3	437	.22	.94	250	−.05	.99	115	−.06	.97	150	−.29	.90	24	−1.14	1.00
Risk index[a]															
24 months	535	1.39	1.70	294	1.68	1.85	130	2.03	2.29	178	2.20	2.05	29	4.34	2.62
36 months	539	1.45	1.68	301	1.88	1.96	129	1.95	2.28	178	2.46	2.05	29	4.31	2.38
54 months	483	1.47	1.72	279	1.91	2.00	121	2.15	2.32	161	2.54	2.10	28	4.68	2.58
Grade 1	463	1.37	1.66	265	1.77	1.95	119	2.08	2.36	160	2.38	1.97	27	4.33	2.48
Grade 3	474	1.35	1.58	273	1.91	1.89	121	2.02	2.23	158	2.37	2.05	28	4.04	2.36
Child characteristics															
Cognitive composite															
24 months	518	94.13	14.2	286	92.43	14.2	128	90.14	14.2	172	89.49	15.5	27	81.22	13.7
36 months	531	98.60	12.3	296	96.61	11.9	127	94.66	13.3	176	92.95	13.7	28	86.04	10.1
54 months	480	100.90	12.3	275	98.36	12.2	120	97.93	13.7	159	94.88	13.5	28	83.70	14.6
Grade 1	456	106.20	10.5	260	104.20	11.6	117	104.80	11.0	155	101.90	11.6	26	95.00	12.5
Grade 3	443	108.60	11.3	254	105.70	12.2	114	106.50	11.2	150	104.00	12.1	26	96.16	12.7

Table 9. (Contd.)

		Aggression Trajectory Group														
		1			2			3			4			5	
	N	Mean	SD	N	Mean	SD	N	Mean	SD	N	Mean	SD	N	Mean	SD
Child-care characteristics																
Child-care quality																
24 months	296	2.86	.57	186	2.79	.52	64	2.78	.56	91	2.74	.56	10	2.41	.65
36 months	311	2.82	.46	198	2.80	.47	60	2.84	.44	101	2.76	.47	17	2.75	.47
54 months	395	3.00	.57	220	2.98	.56	95	3.07	.53	117	2.86	.58	20	2.99	.53
Mean hours of care																
24 months	543	20.53	14.3	301	21.61	14.7	130	16.95	14.9	180	19.12	14.5	29	15.84	13.5
36 months	543	25.30	17.5	301	26.86	17.1	130	20.10	18.2	180	24.84	18.2	29	21.27	16.8
54 months	535	30.76	16.7	297	31.98	16.8	130	27.81	17.2	179	31.86	17.00	29	29.09	15.5
In center (proportion)																
24 months	543	.25		301	.28		130	.23		180	.22		29	.21	
36 months	543	.34		301	.31		130	.27		180	.33		29	.38	
54 months	535	.57		297	.61		130	.62		179	.58		29	.72	

Note.—Groups 1 and 2 are low in aggression; group 3 is moderate in aggression and declines steeply; group 4 is moderate in aggression and declines slightly; and group 5 is high in aggression.

[a]Scaled to 9.

TABLE 10

PROPORTION MEETING EACH CRITERION FOR THE RISK INDEX BY AGGRESSION
TRAJECTORY GROUP

	Aggression Trajectory Group				
	1	2	3	4	5
	Proportion	Proportion	Proportion	Proportion	Proportion
Minority	.19	.21	.27	.24	.47
Maternal Education (<12 years)	.06	.09	.14	.11	.20
Authoritarian	.18	.21	.24	.26	.67
Poverty: income/needs <2.0					
6–24 months (ever)	.36	.46	.45	.49	.83
24 months	.25	.30	.28	.31	.67
36 months	.26	.37	.33	.45	.70
54 months	.23	.34	.34	.41	.72
Grade 1	.18	.31	.29	.40	.64
Grade 3	.15	.30	.24	.30	.60
Single parent					
1–24 months (ever)	.16	.20	.20	.24	.50
24 months	.12	.12	.18	.20	.40
36 months	.13	.15	.20	.24	.33
54 months	.13	.14	.23	.23	.34
Grade 1	.15	.17	.24	.23	.36
Grade 3	.13	.20	.25	.24	.38
4+children in household					
6–24 months (ever)	.07	.10	.06	.10	.10
24 months	.06	.08	.05	.10	.10
36 months	.06	.10	.07	.10	.13
54 months	.08	.10	.10	.12	.17
Grade 1	.09	.10	.11	.14	.19
Grade 3	.11	.12	.12	.10	.17
Maternal depression (CESD >16)					
6–24 months (ever)	.23	.30	.46	.48	.73
24 months	.12	.16	.19	.33	.59
36 months	.09	.18	.22	.32	.45
54 months	.14	.24	.19	.35	.59
Grade 1	.11	.18	.19	.26	.35
Grade 3	.11	.21	.21	.30	.44
Insensitive parenting (bottom quartile on maternal sensitivity)					
6–24 months (ever)	.56	.57	.50	.42	.73
24 months	.22	.24	.30	.35	.61
36 months	.28	.31	.24	.43	.76
54 months	.30	.31	.40	.45	.68
Grade 1	.22	.24	.28	.34	.58
Grade 3	.22	.33	.27	.51	.60

Table 10. (Contd.)

	Aggression Trajectory Group				
	1	2	3	4	5
	Proportion	Proportion	Proportion	Proportion	Proportion
Unstimulating home environment (bottom quartile on HOME)					
6–24 months (ever)	.31	.57	.65	.68	.93
24 months	.19	.25	.38	.35	.69
36 months	.19	.26	.28	.37	.69
54 months	.22	.31	.36	.46	.86
Grade 1	.21	.30	.33	.45	.86
Grade 3	.19	.29	.27	.37	.72

Note. — Groups 1 and 2 are low in aggression; group 3 is moderate in aggression and declines steeply; group 4 is moderate in aggression and declines slightly; and group 5 is high in aggression.

characteristics did not differ significantly among the five aggression trajectories. Thus, these analyses suggest that the group differences observed in the analyses of family, child, and child-care characteristics in the first two years of life were maintained during the child's next 6 years. Overall, family variables were relatively stable and this is illustrated in Figure 2, which shows the average number of risk factors from 24 months through third grade for the five aggression trajectories. This figure makes it clear that risk was very stable and that the high-aggression trajectory group experienced

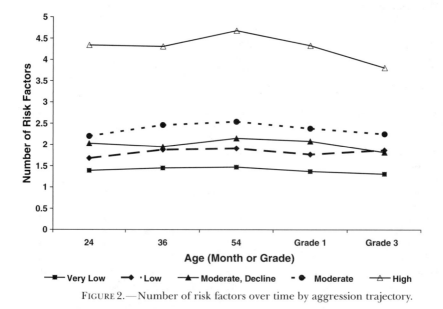

FIGURE 2.—Number of risk factors over time by aggression trajectory.

TABLE 11

TRAJECTORY GROUP DIFFERENCES IN LONGITUDINAL ANALYSES OF FAMILY, CHILD AND CHILD-CARE CHARACTERISTICS BETWEEN 2 YEARS AND THIRD GRADE: SIGNIFICANCE TESTS FOR OVERALL GROUP COMPARISONS AND A PRIORI GROUP CONTRASTS

Predictor	Model Without Covariates						Model With Covariates					
	Group	3 vs. 1,2	4 vs. 1,2	5 vs. 1,2	4 vs. 3	5 vs. 4	Group	3 vs. 1,2	4 vs. 1,2	5 vs.1,2	4 vs. 3	5 vs. 4
	F or χ^2	Effect Size	Effect Size	Effect Size	Effect Size	Effect Size	F	Effect Size	Effect Size	Effect Size	Effect Size	Effect Size
Demographics												
Income group main effect	14.1***	−.13	−.34***	−.94***	−.21	−.60**	3.9***	−.02	−.16*	−.39*	−.14	−.23
Group × age	1.2						1.6					
Partner[a] group main effect	14.4**	.64	.55**	.25***	.87	2.25*	3.7					
Group × age	2.6						1.1					
Family and Maternal												
Maternal sensitivity group main	14.8***	−.13	−.33***	−1.03***	−.21*	−.70***	4.8***	−.02	−.19**	−.61***	−.17	−.42*
Group × age	.9						1.6					
HOME total group main	29.4***	−.24**	−.40***	−1.48***	−.16	−1.07***	14.5***	−.15	−.25***	−1.07***	−.11	−.82***
Group × age	.9						.6					
Maternal depression group main	30.3***	.24**	.54***	.97***	.29**	.44*	21.5***	.21*	.47***	.73***	.26*	.26
Group × age	.2						.1					
Risk group main effect	23.3***	.21*	.37***	1.4***	.16	1.07***						
Group × age	.8											
Child-care characteristics												
Quality—group main effect	1.7						.4					
Group × age	1.4						0.8					
Center care—group main	2.1						2.0					
Group × age	3.9						2.3					

63

Table 11. (Contd.)

Predictor	Model Without Covariates						Model With Covariates					
	Group F or χ^2	3 vs. 1,2 Effect Size	4 vs. 1,2 Effect Size	5 vs. 1,2 Effect Size	4 vs. 3 Effect Size	5 vs. 4 Effect Size	Group F	3 vs. 1,2 Effect Size	4 vs. 1,2 Effect Size	5 vs.1,2 Effect Size	4 vs. 3 Effect Size	5 vs. 4 Effect Size
Total hours/week—group	4.4**	−.36***	−.11	−.26	.25*	−.15	3.4**	−.26***	−.04	−.1	−.30**	−.06
Group × age	2.3						1.6					
Cognitive												
Cognitive composite	13.7***	−.22*	−.33***	−1.0***	−.1	−.67***	2.9*	−.12	−.15	−.48**	−.03	−.33
Group × age	1.8						.8					

Note.—Groups 1 and 2 are low in aggression; group 3 is moderate in aggression and declines steeply; group 4 is moderate in aggression and declines slightly; and group 5 is high in aggression.

Covariates in second model include ethnicity (white/ not white), gender, maternal education, partner in household, and natural log of income/needs ratio.

Covariates are not included in analysis of risk because risk index created from these covariates.

The values listed under group are F-ratio, except for partner, proportion epochs in center care, and center care, which are χ^2. The significance levels under pair-wise comparisons are from t tests except for partner, proportion epochs in center care, which are χ^2.

[a]Effect sizes for categorical variables are reported as the increase (if greater than 1)/decrease (if less than 1) in the odds ratio.

*p <.05.

**p <.01.

***p <.001.

especially high levels of family risk consistently through third grade in comparison to children in the low and moderate-aggression trajectories, with large effect sizes evident (see Table 11). However, the specific hypothesis linking changes in risk to changes in patterns of aggression in the moderate and steeply declining group and the moderate slightly declining aggression group was not supported. As can be seen in Figure 2, these two groups were reasonably similar in risk parameters and changes in risk did not parallel decreases in aggression for the moderate and steeply declining group between 36 and 54 months.

Next, the longitudinal analyses were conducted after including demographic characteristics as covariates in all analyses and other child-care characteristics in analyses of child-care experiences. Results are shown on the right side of Table 11, listing the test statistic for the omnibus tests and effect sizes for specific contrasts if the omnibus test was significant. After adjusting for demographic characteristics, the five trajectory groups continued to show significant differences on family income, maternal sensitivity, stimulation in the home environment, maternal depressive symptoms, child cognition, and hours per week in child care. Again, significant differences were observed in the aggression group main effects, but not in patterns of change over time. This indicates that the five groups differed consistently between 24 months and third grade on these risk factors.

The contrasts showed similar patterns of differences after adjusting for demographic characteristics as were observed in the initial analyses. Although the magnitude of the differences was smaller, the effect sizes still ranged from small to large. Of particular interest, children in the moderate- and high-aggression trajectory groups experienced less maternal sensitivity, less stimulation, and their mothers reported feeling more depressed over time, than mothers of children in the two low-aggression trajectories. Effect sizes were small to modest in the contrasts between the moderate- and low-aggression trajectories and moderate to large in contrasts between the high and low-aggression trajectories. For example, stimulation in the home showed a small, but significant difference ($d = .25$) when the moderate and low-aggression trajectories were compared, and a much larger difference ($d = 1.07$) in the contrast between the high- and low-aggression trajectories. Children in the high-aggression trajectory group also showed lower cognitive functioning over time than children in the low-aggression trajectory groups ($d = .48$). Although there were minimal differences on family variables in the contrasts between the two moderate-aggression trajectory groups (steeply declining, slightly declining), there were more substantial differences between the family environments experienced by children in the high and moderate (slightly declining) aggression trajectories. Children who were rated high on aggression over time also experienced less maternal sensitivity ($d = .42$) and stimulation at home ($d = .82$)

65

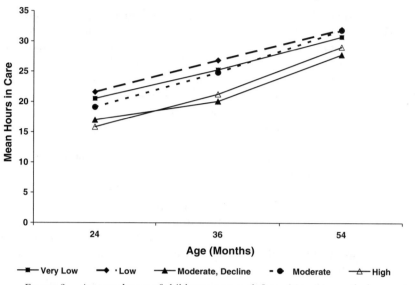

FIGURE 3.—Average hours of child care per week from 24 to 54 months by aggression trajectory.

than children whose aggression was relatively stable, but only at a moderate level.

Hours in child care also varied by trajectory group, when demographic and other child-care parameters were controlled. Children in the moderate, steeply declining aggression group experienced fewer hours in child care than children in the two low-aggression groups ($d = .26$) and than children in the moderate, but only slightly declining group ($d = .30$). Hours of care by trajectory group are displayed in Figure 3.

SUMMARY AND CONCLUSIONS

These analyses make it clear that trajectory membership is associated with differences in both early levels of risk and continuing levels of risk. This was true when individual risk variables were examined and when a cumulative risk index was substituted for specific measures. Both family demographics and more proximal indicators of family context and parent–child interaction were associated with these different risk trajectories, initially and over time. In addition, there were significantly higher proportions of boys in the higher risk trajectory groups. With few exceptions, family characteristics associated with trajectory membership, including income, stimulation in the home, maternal sensitivity, and maternal reports of depressive symptoms were quite stable. No variables showed age by trajectory inter-actions that would indicate different patterns of change over time. Children in the two lowest aggression trajectories and in the moderate, relatively stable aggression trajectory were in more hours of child care than children in the moderate and steeply declining group, but neither child-care quality nor time in center care were associated with trajectory membership. The next chapter addresses how well these trajectories predict outcomes at third grade.

V. PERSON-CENTERED AGGRESSION TRAJECTORIES AND THIRD GRADE OUTCOMES

In this chapter we ask whether academic and social–emotional outcomes in third grade differ among groups of children who showed distinct developmental trajectories of aggressive behavior from 2 years to third grade according to maternal ratings. We examine how well these trajectories predict to a range of outcomes at third grade reflecting social adjustment at school, in the family, and in the peer group, as well as academic competence and achievement. Indicators of competence are included along with measures of behavior problems. Although we focus primarily on teacher reports of social competence and behavior problems so as to minimize reporter bias, two maternal report measures of parenting are included. We also include children's self-reports of their friendships and peer relationships along with independent observations of children's actual behavior in school. Again we examine indicators of competence and of problem behavior.

Although it is logical to emphasize externalizing problems as the outcome of interest as has been done in earlier studies using aggression trajectories to predict later functioning (e.g., Broidy et al., 2003), these studies involved older children and focused primarily on delinquency and serious aggression in adolescence as outcomes. Because the children in our study are only 9 years old at follow-up a focus on delinquency is not appropriate. In addition, early and persistent aggression has been associated with a wide range of negative outcomes, many less serious than delinquency. Thus, we include not only measures of externalizing problems, but also internalizing problems and inattention/impulsivity. In the clinical literature, it is well known that these problems co-occur (e.g., Angold, Costello, & Erklani, 1999; Caron & Rutter, 1991; Jensen, Martin, & Cantwell, 1997). Because we are studying a large community sample, we also examine adjustment in third grade, broadly defined, to determine whether these trajectories of aggressive behavior are differentially associated with different patterns of outcomes as well as different levels of problem severity. For example, even in the absence of serious aggression or externalizing problems, children in the moderate and only slightly declining aggression group may still have problems that are reflected in lower levels of academic and social competence relative to those in the two low-aggression trajectory groups.

We also ask whether the moderate but steeply declining trajectory group (group 3) shows any residual problems in third grade or whether their early aggression was indeed merely a reflection of age-related and transient difficulties as perceived by their mothers. These children are not expected to show *high* levels of externalizing behavior in third grade, but they may show more subtle problems with academic performance or peer relations. In addition, it is of particular interest to compare the two moderate aggression groups with different developmental trajectories (i.e., the steeply declining group and the slightly declining group), as they may be expected to show different patterns of functioning in grade 3, reflecting differences in self-regulation and control of impulses. Similarly, the two higher-aggression groups (high; moderate, slightly declining) may have differing outcomes that reflect either qualitative or quantitative differences in functioning. For example, they may show the same pattern of functioning, but at different levels of severity, or different patterns of functioning, suggesting different types of problems at third grade. It is assumed that both of these groups will differ significantly from the two low-aggression groups on a range of third grade outcomes across measures, settings, and reporters. However, the moderate, slightly declining aggression group may be at risk primarily for learning and attentional problems, whereas the high-aggression group may be at risk for problems controlling aggression and hostility, and also for more serious problems with peers, as well as for attentional problems.

ANALYSIS PLAN

Due to the large number of third grade outcomes of interest, the analysis plan involved first testing whether the trajectory groups differed on blocks of conceptually related outcome variables before examining each outcome individually. Multivariate analyses of covariance (MANCOVAs) tested whether the trajectory groups differed on blocks of continuous, approximately normally distributed outcomes. Many of the indicators of behavior problems and peer competence were quite skewed and, therefore, were categorized for these analyses, depending on whether the child scored in a "problematic" range or in the "normal" range. Logistic regression analyses were conducted on categorical variables. To get a clear picture of how outcomes varied with trajectory group, only gender was controlled in the first set of analyses and gender and demographic characteristics were controlled in the second set of analyses. The covariates included third grade family income (log transformed), maternal education, whether the mother had a partner in the household, and the child's ethnicity (coded as white/non-Hispanic or not).

There was a step-down plan for interpreting results. An omnibus test was conducted for each set of variables. It was followed by separate univariate tests for each outcome only if the omnibus test was significant. When significant trajectory group differences were observed in the univariate tests, a priori contrasts among the groups followed. The contrasts involved the same comparisons as previously described: the two low-aggression groups (1 and 2) were compared with the two higher-aggression groups (4 and 5) individually to address differences in the sequelae at third grade of being on low and higher trajectories of aggression from 24 months to third grade. Because the two higher-trajectory groups showed different levels of aggression, they were examined separately in these analyses. Differences between the two low- and two higher-trajectory groups are, however, expected on indices of academic achievement, social competence, behavior problems, and peer relations. These contrasts will be presented first. Next, we report on differences at third grade between the two higher-trajectory groups, following the parallel pattern of relatively lower (i.e., moderate, slightly declining) in comparison to higher aggression (high stable). Because these groups differ in level of aggression, the high-trajectory group is expected to be functioning more poorly across social and academic domains in third grade than is the moderately aggressive, slightly declining trajectory group.

The fourth set of contrasts examines whether children who start out at different levels of mother-rated aggression in early childhood (low or moderate), but are all rated low in aggression by school entry, show any differences at third grade. These groups are not expected to show major differences by third grade in line with the assumption that the moderate and steeply declining group was showing age-related aggression associated with the emergence of autonomy. However, it is possible that subtle residual effects remain.

Finally, the two moderate groups (steeply declining and slightly declining) are compared. These groups started out with similar levels of early aggression as perceived by mothers, but their trajectories diverged sharply between 36 and 54 months, suggesting that these two groups should evidence differences in social competence, behavior problems, academic achievement, and peer relations at third grade. As already noted we are assuming that the age-related decline reflects more transient problems whereas a moderate level of aggression that declines only slightly over the course of early development should be a risk factor for problems across domains of functioning at third grade.

When significant effects were obtained in the a priori contrasts, effect sizes were computed. The effect sizes for the continuous variables were computed as the difference between the adjusted means divided by the estimated standard error under the model, the root mean squared error. Descriptive statistics on outcome variables are summarized in Table 12 and analysis results are presented in Table 13. In terms of interpreting the effect sizes, the value of $-.28$ in the column labeled 4 vs. 1, 2 and the row labeled "cognitive" in Table 13 means that the children in the moderate aggression group score .28 standard deviations below the children in the low-aggression groups. This effect size, d, represents the difference between the means in terms of standard deviation units, and effect sizes of .3 are considered modest, .5 moderate, and .8 large (Cohen, 1988). The effect sizes for categorical variables were computed as odds ratios. An odds ratio of 1 means the estimated proportion of children in that category was the same for the two groups involved in the contrast. An odds ratio larger than 1 means that the estimated proportion in the first group listed in that column was higher than in the second group listed in the column. For example, the odds ratio in the column labeled 3 vs. 1, 2 and the row labeled school performance indicates that children in the moderate, steeply declining aggression trajectory were 1.51 times more likely to be classified as having problems with school performance than children in the two low-aggression trajectories.

RESULTS

Descriptive Statistics and Group Main Effects

As Table 12 indicates, the outcomes were divided into seven categories, representing the source and/or construct being measured. These will be described briefly and main effects noted for comparisons with gender as the covariate and with gender and demographic characteristics as covariates. Then the a priori contrasts will be discussed individually once the omnibus results are presented.

Cognitive and Academic Achievement

During laboratory visits at third grade, children were administered the Woodcock–Johnson Cognitive and Achievement tests (Woodcock & Johnson, 1989, 1990). Composite scores were created by computing the mean of the standard scores from each battery. The cognitive score was the mean of the standard scores obtained on the Picture Vocabulary, Memory for Words, and Memory for Sentences subtests. The achievement composite was the mean of the Letter-Word, Passage Comprehension, and Applied Problem

71

TABLE 12

THIRD GRADE ACADEMIC, SOCIAL, AND PEER OUTCOMES BY AGGRESSION TRAJECTORY GROUP

	Group 1 Very Low 473		Group 2 Low 269		Group 3 Moderate/ Decline 120		Group 4 Moderate 159		Group 5 High 28	
	Mean	SD	Mean	SD	Mean	SD	Mean	SD	Mean	SD
Academic outcomes—standardized tests										
Cognitive composite	108.6	11.3	105.7	12.2	106.5	11.2	104.0	12.1	96.2	12.7
Achievement composite	115.7	11.7	111.8	13.7	113.9	13.2	110.3	15.3	103.7	15.9
Parenting-mother report										
Harsh discipline	24.0	3.7	24.7	3.8	24.5	4.0	25.1	3.8	27.3	3.7
Mother–child conflict	13.6	5.1	17.3	5.7	16.1	5.5	20.1	5.8	23.9	5.7
Child social competence at school										
Teacher rating of social skills	105.4	14.2	101.0	13.0	101.6	14.9	97.9	14.9	88.8	12.6
Teacher–child closeness	33.6	5.0	33.3	5.0	32.5	5.5	32.3	5.3	29.5	5.4
Teacher reports—school problems										
School performance	3.6	0.8	3.4	0.9	3.4	1.0	3.0	1.0	2.6	0.9
Below 3rd grade level	18.3%		28.5%		31.3%		43.8%		57.7%	
Externalizing	49.4	8.5	52.2	8.9	51.7	9.3	54.1	10.4	61.5	9.7
>59	12.8%		19.0%		20.9%		26.7%		57.7%	
Internalizing	50.8	9.1	51.6	9.6	51.7	9.2	52.8	10.4	56.4	9.4
>59	18.0%		22.7%		20.9%		28.8%		38.5%	
ADHD or ODD (Y/N)	10.0%		14.5%		15.6%		26.7%		42.3%	
ADHD hyperactive (Y/N)	2.9%		7.7%		9.2%		13.0%		26.9%	
ADHD inattentive (Y/N)	7.6%		8.5%		9.2%		20.6%		32.0%	
Oppositional disorder (Y/N)	4.0%		4.9%		4.6%		6.8%		19.2%	
Teacher–child conflict	10.3	5.2	12.0	6.1	11.8	6.1	13.1	6.6	17.2	7.5
>1 SD above the mean	10.6%		15.9%		18.2%		22.8%		50.0%	
Observed: disruptive at lunch[a]	4.9%		7.6%		7.8%		5.5%		22.7%	
Observed: disruptive in class[a]	0.7	2.6	0.7	2.0	0.6	1.7	1.3	3.5	2.7	4.9
>0	20.1%		23.1%		23.2%		30.8%		50.0%	
Observed behaviors at school										
Disengaged/off task	19.2	8.4	20.2	8.2	20.3	8.5	21.6	8.2	21.8	7.7
Positive involvement	20.7	2.4	20.3	2.3	20.2	2.6	19.8	2.6	19.0	2.9
Positive with peers at lunch	5.9	1.6	5.8	1.7	5.4	1.7	5.6	1.7	5.6	1.0
Teacher reports of peer relationships										
Asocial with peers	0.4	0.5	0.3	0.4	0.4	0.5	0.4	0.5	0.4	0.4
Upper 25th percentile	19.7%		19.0%		26.4%		28.1%		23.1%	
Excluded by peers	0.3	0.5	0.4	0.5	0.4	0.5	0.4	0.6	0.6	0.6
Upper 25th percentile	19.0%		25.3%		29.4%		33.8%		46.2%	
Peer victimization	0.1	0.2	0.2	0.3	0.2	0.3	0.2	0.4	0.3	0.3
Upper 25th percentile	23.2%		38.2%		35.5%		40.4%		61.5%	
Relational aggression	0.3	0.4	0.4	0.4	0.4	0.4	0.4	0.4	0.6	0.5
Upper 25th percentile	13.8%		23.2%		21.1%		21.9%		34.6%	
Number of close friends	2.6	0.6	2.6	0.6	2.6	0.6	2.4	0.7	2.1	0.5
<3	37.1%		38.9%		38.2%		47.9%		80.8%	

Table 12. (Contd.)

	Group 1 Very Low 473		Group 2 Low 269		Group 3 Moderate/ Decline 120		Group 4 Moderate 159		Group 5 High 28	
	Mean	SD	Mean	SD	Mean	SD	Mean	SD	Mean	SD
Child reports of peer relationships										
Loneliness	26.9	8.7	28.8	9.5	29.7	10.6	30.5	10.1	34.0	12.8
>1 SD above the mean	12.0%		18.8%		18.6%		24.5%		36.0%	
Friendship quality	4.0	0.6	4.0	0.7	3.9	0.7	4.0	0.6	3.9	0.8
Perceived victimization score	1.7	0.7	1.9	0.8	1.8	0.7	2.0	0.9	2.2	1.0
>1 SD above the mean	7.9%		18.6%		11.9%		19.2%		18.5%	
Engagement in bullying	1.1	0.3	1.2	0.5	1.2	0.5	1.3	0.4	1.4	0.7
>1 SD above the mean	13.2%		24.5%		24.2%		35.4%		41.7%	
Hostile intent instrumental	0.2	0.3	0.2	0.3	0.2	0.3	0.2	0.3	0.4	0.4
>1 SD above the mean	17.4%		22.8%		15.8%		18.0%		40.7%	
Hostile intent relational	0.3	0.2	0.3	0.3	0.3	0.2	0.4	0.2	0.5	0.3
>1 SD above the mean	2.5%		6.3%		3.5%		3.3%		25.9%	

[a]Independent observations, not teacher report.

Scale standard scores. As shown in Table 13, group differences were obtained in the MANCOVA, and in the follow-up ANCOVAs for the cognitive and achievement outcomes when gender only was controlled. Despite some large effect sizes in the a priori contrasts, the five trajectory groups did not differ when demographic characteristics were controlled (see first set of rows in Table 13).

Maternal Reports of Parenting

Two maternal report measures were included in these analyses. Mothers were asked about their approach to discipline and about conflict with the study child. Again there were overall main effects of group in the MANCOVA and significant differences across groups on both these variables in the ANCOVAs with only gender controlled. With all the covariates controlled, the group main effect remained significant, but only mother–child conflict still differentiated trajectory groups. Harsh discipline was no longer significant in the more conservative model.

Teacher Reports of Social Competence

Third grade teachers reported on children's social competence with peers on the Social Skills Rating System (Social Skills Total Standard Score)

TABLE 13

TRAJECTORY GROUP COMPARISONS ON ACADEMIC, SOCIAL, AND BEHAVIOR PROBLEM OUTCOMES AND MATERNAL REPORTS OF PARENTING

| | Model with Gender as Only Covariate | | | | | | Model with Gender and Demographic Characteristics | | | | | |
| | | Effect Sizes for Selected Contrasts | | | | | | Effect Sizes for Selected Contrasts | | | | |
Continuous outcomes	Group Test F	3 vs. 1,2 d	4 vs. 1,2 d	5 vs. 1,2 d	4 vs. 3 d	5 vs. 4 d	Group Test F	3 vs. 1,2 d	4 vs. 1,2 d	5 vs. 1,2 d	4 vs. 3 d	5 vs. 4 d
Academic outcomes	6.1***						1.7					
Cognitive	11.0***	−.06	−.28**	−.96***	−.22	−.68*						
Achievement	9.4***	.02	−.25**	−.74***	−.27*	−.49*						
Parenting-mother report	34.1***						30.1***					
Harsh discipline	6.7***	.06	.22*	.77***	.16	.55**	1.7					
Mother–child conflict	63.7***	.14	.89***	1.63***	.74***	.74***	61.6***	.19	.92***	1.69***	.73***	.77***
Social competence at school	7.8***						4.3***					
Social Skills	14.9***	−.12	−.38***	−1.03***	−.26*	−.66**	7.8***	−.07	−.28*	−.74***	−.21	−.46*
Teacher–child closeness	3.8**	−.13	−.18	−.68**	−.05	−.49*	2.3					
Behavior in school	2.5*						1.3					
Off task—class	2.0											
Positive involvement—class	5.4***	−.13	−.27**	−.74***	−.14	−.47*						
Positive with peers—lunch	2.3											
Categorical outcomes	χ^2	OR	OR	OR	OR	OR	χ^2	OR	OR	OR	OR	OR
Behavior problems at school	44.0***						26.9***					
School performance[a]	47.2***	1.51***	2.59***	4.50*	1.71*	1.73	17.5**	1.31	2.16***	1.71	1.65	.79
Externalizing[a]	36.9***	1.45	2.01**	7.69***	1.38	3.83***	20.5***	1.39	1.76*	4.70***	1.26	2.67*
Internalizing[a]	10.7*	1.03	1.57*	2.38*	1.52	1.52	5.1					
ADHD/ODD[a]	26.5***	1.22	2.41***	4.41***	1.98*	1.83	14.2**	1.26	2.29***	2.49*	1.82	1.09
Teacher–child conflict[a]	24.7***	1.36	1.79*	5.66***	1.31	3.16**	10.2*	1.28	1.47	3.18***	1.14	2.16
Disruptive at lunch[a]	6.9						5.2					
Disruptive in class[a]	11.2*	1.01	1.48	3.12*	1.46	2.11	4.8					

74

TABLE 13. (Contd.)

	Model with Gender as Only Covariate						Model with Gender and Demographic Characteristics					
		Effect Sizes for Selected Contrasts						Effect Sizes for Selected Contrasts				
	Group Test χ^2	3 vs. 1,2 OR	4 vs. 1,2 OR	5 vs. 1,2 OR	4 vs. 3 OR	5 vs. 4 OR	Group Test χ^2	3 vs. 1,2 OR	4 vs. 1,2 OR	5 vs. 1,2 OR	4 vs. 3 OR	5 vs. 4 OR
Teacher-report of peer relationships	30.5***						16.2**					
Asocial[a]	5.4						3.6					
Excluded[a]	18.9***	1.45	1.77**	2.92**	1.22	1.65	7.4					
Victimized[a]	33.1***	1.25	1.54**	3.59***	1.23	2.33	19.2***	1.29	1.37	2.41*	1.05	1.76
Relational aggression[a]	17.8**	1.29	1.37	2.77*	1.06	2.03	11.0*	1.21	1.24	1.74	1.03	1.40
Fewer than 3 friends[a]	23.1***	1.01	1.50*	6.83***	1.49	4.55**	16.8**	.92	1.38	5.67***	1.50	4.11**
Self-report of peer relationships	22.9***						13.3*					
Loneliness[a]	21.2***	1.32	1.88**	3.38**	1.43	1.79	5.9					
Friendship quality	1.0						0.5					
Victimization[a]	23.9***	1.00	1.76*	1.76	1.76	1.00	19.0**	.95	1.61	1.26	1.70	.79
Bully[a]	22.0***	1.40	2.44**	3.05	1.74	1.25	19.4***	1.23	2.55***	3.54	2.07	1.39
Hostile instrumental[a]	9.9*	.72	.84	2.49*	1.16	2.96*	9.3					
Hostile relational[a]	22.2***	.90	.86	9.08***	.95	10.61***	16.0**	.82	.74	6.12***	.90	8.25**

Note.—Groups 1 and 2 are low in aggression; group 3 is moderate in aggression and declines steeply; group 4 is moderate in aggression and declines slightly; group 5 is high in aggression

*p < .05.
**p < .01.
***p < .001.
[a] Logistic regression.

75

and on their own relationship with the study child on the Closeness scale of the Student–Teacher Relationship Scale. The overall MANCOVA and follow-up tests were significant when only gender was controlled. With all the demographic covariates in the model, group differences in social skills remained significant, but teacher–child closeness did not. In each comparison, children on the higher-aggression trajectories were less socially skilled than those on the lower-aggression trajectories.

Observational Measures of Classroom Behavior: Attention, Positive Affect, and Positive Engagement

Observers coded frequencies of off-task and disengaged behavior in the classroom and this was composited to reflect "off-task" behavior. A positive engagement score was derived from 7-point ratings of self-reliance, paying attention, and positive relationship with teacher in the classroom. Positive behavior with peers at lunch was a composite of two 7-point ratings: positive affect and social-cooperative behavior. These outcomes were treated as continuous variables because their distributions were approximately normal. Summary statistics for each outcome by trajectory group are presented in Table 12. A multivariate analysis of variance controlling for gender indicated that the groups differed on these observational measures as well. However, the univariate tests indicated that groups differed only in positive engagement in the classroom. Group differences were not statistically significant when demographic characteristics were added as covariates.

Teacher Reports and Observations of Behavior Problems

Logistic regressions were used to examine categorical indicators from teacher reports and observations of behavior problems at school. Logistic regression models were tested because these measures were all highly skewed toward a low level of problems and were, therefore, recoded to reflect no to low levels of problems (0) in comparison with higher levels of problems (1). Poor school performance was operationalized as a teacher rating of "below grade level" in academic subjects. Internalizing and externalizing behavior as rated by teachers on the TRF was recoded to 0 when children were within one standard deviation of the mean ($T = 59$ or lower $= 0$) and 1 when they were one standard deviation or more above the mean ($T = 60$ or greater $= 1$). In addition, symptom ratings on the Disruptive Behavior Questionnaire were coded as 1 if children scored high ("pretty much" or "very much" a problem) on 6 symptoms of inattention, 6 symptoms of hyperactivity/impulsivity, or 5 symptoms of oppositional defiant disorder, consistent with DSM-IV (American Psychiatric Association, 1994) symptom criteria for ADHD and ODD; otherwise the score was 0. Because so few children met any of these criteria, these measures were collapsed into one disruptive behavior problem index. Teacher–child conflict on the Student–Teacher Relationship questionnaire was likewise skewed and coded as present or absent; children scoring more than one standard deviation above the mean were scored a 1 reflecting some conflict.

Two observational measures of disruptive behavior were obtained when research assistants visited the school in third grade. Disruptive behavior at lunch was scored present when the child was out of control, annoying other children, or not following rules and defying the teacher. Disruptive behavior in the classroom was similarly rated as present when children ignored or actively defied the teacher, annoyed other children, or behaved inappropriately by calling attention to themselves when they were supposed to be working or sitting quietly. Since only minimal levels of disruptive behavior were observed in these third grade classrooms, any indication was coded as a 1. Most children received 0 scores on this measure.

The omnibus test of these seven variables indicated that group membership was highly predictive of these outcomes in the analyses with only gender controlled and also with the more extensive set of demographic covariates. This test was a logistic regression in which the outcome variable reflected whether the child scored in the problematic range on one or more of the seven measures. Follow-up logistic regressions of each of the seven measures of behavior problems at school indicated that groups differed on all measures except observations of disruptive behavior at lunch in analyses with gender as the covariate and the groups continued to differ on four of the seven outcomes in analyses with demographic characteristics as covariates (poor school performance, externalizing problems, ADHD/ODD symptoms, and teacher–child conflict).

Teacher Ratings of Peer Problems

Teachers also rated peer problems on a questionnaire assessing children's asocial behavior, exclusion by peers, victimization by peers, and use of relational aggression; they also reported on the number of friends study children had in the classroom. Because of skewed distributions, these variables were dichotomized: the top 25% of the sample was considered problematic on the peer variables. Teacher reports of fewer than three classroom friends were recoded as problematic, reflecting the bottom quarter of the distribution on this variable.

The omnibus test of these five variables was significant in analyses with only gender and with additional demographic characteristics as covariates.

Again, this test was a logistic regression in which children were considered as problematic if they scored in the problem range on one or more of these outcomes. The five trajectory groups showed significant differences in the logistic regression for four of the five outcomes in analyses that adjusted for gender only and on three of the five outcomes in analyses that adjusted for gender and family demographics (victimization, relational aggression, and friendlessness), as can be seen in Table 13.

Self-Reports of Peer Problems and Friendship Quality

During laboratory visits in third grade, children were administered several measures of peer competence including the Loneliness and Friendship Quality questionnaires, and vignettes assessing hostile attributional biases from which instrumental and relational aggression bias scores were derived. Perceptions of being victimized were assessed as were self-reports of bullying others. The omnibus test was significant in both sets of analyses. Univariate tests indicated that the groups differed on all measures except self-reported friendship quality when gender was the only covariate and on victimization, bullying, and hostile relational measures when gender and demographic characteristics were included as covariates.

A Priori Contrasts

Low-Aggression Versus High-Aggression Groups

The two consistently low-aggression groups were compared with the moderate, slightly declining group in the first set of a priori contrasts (labeled "4 vs. 1, 2") and the high-aggression group (labeled "5 vs. 1, 2") in the second set. Significant differences in the expected direction were obtained on most measures when gender was the only covariate, as can be seen in Table 13. Children in the moderate- and high-aggression groups performed more poorly than children in the two low groups on the Woodcock–Johnson tests of cognitive functioning and academic achievement, and they received lower ratings from teachers on social skills, with effect sizes ranging from modest to large (.25–1.03). Indeed, with only gender controlled, children in the high-aggression trajectory group scored almost a whole standard deviation lower than children in the two low-aggression trajectories on cognitive outcomes and one standard deviation lower on teacher ratings of social skills. Some of these differences, however, were confounded with family demographics. Once these were controlled the high- and moderate-aggression groups no longer differed from the two low-aggression trajectory groups on cognitive or achievement scores, although they continued to receive lower ratings of social skills with small to modest (.28–.74) effect sizes.

Teachers also rated the children on both higher-aggression trajectories as showing more externalizing and internalizing problems, and specifically more DSM-IV symptoms of ADHD and ODD combined, than the children in the two low-trajectory groups. Teacher–child conflict also was rated higher and school performance as lower in both these contrasts. Even with the larger set of covariates controlled, children showing high and stable aggression were 2.5 times more likely to be rated as showing symptoms of ADHD/ODD and 4.7 times more likely to have elevated scores on the externalizing scale of the CBCL than those on the two low-aggression trajectories. The comparable odds ratios for the moderate-aggression trajectory group in comparison to the low-aggressive children were 2.3 for ADHD/ODD symptoms and 1.76 for externalizing. Differences were also in evidence for ratings of teacher–child conflict (high aggression vs. low aggression) and for poor school performance (moderate vs. low aggression). Internalizing problems no longer differentiated the groups with covariates controlled, despite the relatively high odds ratios in the analyses controlling only for gender (1.57 and 2.38).

Independent observations in the third grade classroom indicated that the moderately aggressive and highly aggressive children were also less engaged in constructive classroom activities and the high-aggressive children were observed to be more disruptive than children on the low-aggression trajectories. These variables were no longer significant when all the demographic covariates were controlled. Mothers' ratings were consistent with this assessment of more disruptive behavior: they reported using harsher discipline and having more conflict with third graders in the moderate and high-aggressive trajectory groups than with those in the two low-aggressive trajectory groups. When all the demographic covariates were controlled, mothers of children in the high-aggression trajectory group were still more likely to report more mother–child conflict ($d = 1.69$), as were mothers of children in the moderate aggression group ($d = .92$), when compared with mothers of children in the low-aggression trajectories.

These adjustment differences also were reflected in teacher-reported and self-reported peer relations. Teachers saw children in the two aggressive trajectory groups as more excluded and victimized by peers and as having fewer classroom friends than children in the two low-trajectory groups. The children on the highest-aggression trajectory were also seen by teachers as more likely to engage in relational aggression toward peers than those in the lowest two groups. Children in the two higher-aggression groups also reported feeling more lonely than did children in the two low-aggression groups. Finally, moderately aggressive children reported that they were more likely to be victimized and to bully others than those in the

79

two low-aggression trajectory groups. In contrast, children in the high-aggression group endorsed more aggressive reasons for ambiguous peer events, reflecting more hostile and relational attributional biases. In general, the pattern of results was similar, but the magnitude of the differences between the high-aggression group and the two low groups was larger than that between the moderately aggressive group and the two low groups. Odds ratios for the comparisons between the high- and low-aggression groups ranged from 1.76 to 9.08, whereas odds ratios for the comparisons of moderate- and low-aggression groups ranged from .84 to 2.44, underscoring the large differences between the high- and stable-aggression group and the two low groups when both teacher- and self-reports of peer problems were examined.

After adjusting for demographic characteristics, significant differences between the low-aggression groups and both the moderate- and high-aggression groups were still observed on several of these measures of peer problems, especially between the high-aggressive and low-aggressive trajectory groups. Children in the moderate-aggression group reported that they engaged in bullying more than did children in the low-aggression groups. Children in the high-aggression group were still more likely to offer hostile instrumental and relational aggressive solutions to social problems; they were also rated by teachers as victimized by peers and as having fewer friends in the classroom. Overall, children in the moderate-aggression group appeared to be more picked on by others, whereas those in the high-aggression group appeared to be victimized, but also to initiate more hostile encounters according to teacher- and self-reports.

Moderate- Versus High-Aggression Groups

Although the two higher-aggression groups differed from the two low groups on most measures, the magnitude of the differences and the overall level of aggression were consistent with the possibility that they would also differ from one another in terms of the severity of problems. As can be seen in the 6th column of Table 13 (labeled "4 vs. 5"), when only gender was controlled, children in the highest-aggression trajectory group performed more poorly than children in the moderate group on measures of academic and cognitive functioning; teachers rated them lower in social skills and teacher–child closeness, and higher in externalizing behavior and teacher–child conflict. They were also less engaged in productive classroom activities when observed in school, and teachers rated them as having fewer classroom friends. Mothers also reported using harsher discipline with the children in the high-aggression trajectory and as having more conflict with their child. Finally, the children in the high-aggression trajectory group made more negative attributions toward peers' intentions in ambiguous situations tapping both expectations of hostile instrumental and relational aggression than did children in the moderately aggressive group.

Effect sizes for continuous variables were in the moderate range (.47–.74). Odds ratios for categorical variables were substantial for comparisons on externalizing problems and teacher–child conflict, with high-aggression children 3.83 times more likely to be categorized as showing externalizing problems and 3.16 times more likely to be rated as high in conflict with the teacher than children showing moderate, relatively stable aggression. Indeed, children on the high-aggression trajectory were 2.96 times more likely to select hostile instrumental aggressive solutions to social problems and 10.6 times more likely select hostile relational aggressive solutions than children who were only moderately aggressive. To some degree, these differences were confounded with differences in demographics, as might be expected from differences in the overall risk index. Despite this, with demographics controlled, significant differences remained on measures of mother–child conflict, teacher reports of social skills, externalizing problems, number of classroom friends, and self-reports of hostile relational aggression.

Thus, overall, higher levels of aggression over time predicted different third grade outcomes; those on the higher-aggression trajectories looked worse, often much worse, across a range of competence and behavior problem measures than those on lower trajectories, and this held true not only when examining both the extremes of trajectories of aggressive behavior in this sample (high and low), but also when moderate- and high-aggressive groups were compared.

Low Groups Versus the Moderate and Steeply Declining Group

Recall that the two low groups and the moderate declining group started out with different levels of early aggression, but by 54 months the moderate group was showing a sharp decline in aggression that dropped to almost zero by first grade, making them indistinguishable from the two low groups on later aggression. Although it was unlikely that these children would differ on many third grade outcomes given their low levels of aggression by elementary school age, the possibility of subtle, residual effects of early aggression were explored in these contrasts. As column 2 of Table 13 indicates, these trajectory groups only differed significantly on one variable examined in these analyses, but this was no longer significant when demographics were controlled. These findings lend support to the argument that the aggression observed in the moderate and steeply declining group was indeed age-related and transient.

81

The Moderate and Steeply Declining Group Versus the Moderate and Slightly Declining Group

Although these two groups began with relatively high levels of aggression at 24 and 36 months, their pathways diverged quite clearly at 54 months and beyond, suggesting that despite similar levels of early aggression and no differences in predictors of trajectory membership or early risk, these two groups of children were following quite different developmental pathways with different implications for functioning in third grade. Surprisingly, however, the groups differed on only a few variables in third grade when only gender was controlled and on only one variable with all covariates controlled. Children in the moderate and sharply declining group performed better on the Woodcock–Johnson achievement test, engaged in less conflict with their mothers, and were seen as having better social skills than those in the moderate and only slightly declining trajectory group. Teachers also saw the slightly declining group as performing more poorly in school and as demonstrating more symptoms of ADHD and ODD. Observations of school behavior and measures of behavior with peers did not discriminate between these two trajectory groups. With all covariates controlled only mother–child conflict remained significant, although it is noteworthy that teachers were nearly twice as likely to see the children in the moderate-aggression group as showing symptoms of ADHD/ODD than children in the steeply declining group (odds ratio of 1.82 with covariates).

Follow-Up Analyses

Comparison Between Moderate Group and High Stable Group on Oppositional Behavior

The two higher-aggression trajectory groups differed from the two low groups on almost all measures at the third grade follow-up indicating poorer academic and social functioning at school, more problems with peers at school, and more conflict with their mothers at home. At the same time, these two groups also differed from each other. Children on the high- and stable-aggression trajectory had lower scores on cognitive and achievement measures, teachers rated them as lower in social competence, higher on measures of teacher–child conflict and externalizing problems, and as having fewer friends at school. Independent observations also indicated that the high-aggression group was less engaged in appropriate classroom activities. Other differences suggested more hostility and conflict with parents and peers. Thus, we wondered whether children in the high-aggression trajectory group were showing generally higher levels of disruptive behavior, especially more oppositional and antisocial behavior than children in the moderate group. We explored this by disaggregating the disruptive behavior problem questionnaire and the TRF externalizing scale to examine specific symptoms of oppositional behavior and delinquency at third grade. When the two higher-aggression trajectory groups were compared on symptoms of oppositional behavior (M's = 3.45 and 6.86) and on the TRF Delinquency scale (M's = 55.76 and 62.96), children on the high-aggression trajectory received significantly higher ratings from teachers than did children in the moderate-aggression group ($p < .01$). This may suggest that children in the moderate group are showing primarily poorer self-regulatory skills and attention problems, whereas children in the high-aggression group may be showing more serious problems monitoring aggression and hostility.

Language Competence and Impulse Control as Possible Factors Accounting for Differences Between the Two Moderately Aggressive Groups

The two groups that were rated as showing moderate levels of aggression at 24 months began to diverge in their levels of aggression between 36 months and 54 months. One group was on a steeply declining aggression trajectory, whereas the other group of children remained elevated, showing a smaller decline in aggression through third grade. In considering what processes might account for these different patterns of change in aggression over time, we entertained the hypothesis that children in the steeply declining group might be developing better language skills and self-regulatory strategies during this period that allowed them to deal with frustration in more adaptive ways, whereas children in the moderate and more stable aggression group might be less linguistically skilled and more poorly regulated. To test this hypothesis, we compared the children in these two trajectory groups on measures of language competence and impulse control at 36 and 54 months. The language measures included the Reynell Developmental Language Scale at 36 months and the Preschool Language Scale at 54 months. Contrary to expectation, the groups did not differ on either of these measures indicating that differences in language competence did not account for differences in trajectories.

Several measures of impulse control were also examined. At 36 months, children were observed in a forbidden toy situation where they were instructed to refrain from touching an attractive toy for 3 minutes; active engagement time with the forbidden toy was recorded. At 54 months children were administered a delay of gratification task during which they could choose a small amount of one of their favorite foods immediately or wait for 7 minutes to receive a larger amount. Children were scored as pass/fail based on whether or not they were able to wait for the entire delay period. In addition, at 54 months, children completed a simplified version of the Continuous Performance Test. Children were instructed to push a button when a picture of a chair appeared on a screen and to refrain from pushing when other pictures appeared. Commission errors (incorrect hits) were considered to be impulsive responses. Groups did not differ in their ability to wait to touch the forbidden toy at 36 months. However, by 54 months differences in self-regulation were in evidence. Children in the steeply declining aggression trajectory group made fewer commission errors on the CPT than children in the more stable group (M's = 13.9 and 18.1 respectively $p < .03$) and they were more likely to wait during the delay of gratification task at 54 months (55% waited vs. 39%, $p = .014$), consistent with the hypothesis that decreases in aggression were associated with the emergence of better self-regulatory skills. Thus, children in the steeply declining aggression group were less impulsive than those in the more stable group on both measures of self-regulation at 54 months, but not at 36 months and they did not differ in language competence at either age. Thus, these follow-up hypotheses were partially supported.

A Comment on Sex Differences

Main effects of gender were found on a number of variables examined at third grade, as might be expected. Boys were rated higher than girls on teacher–child conflict, lower on teacher–child closeness, and higher on ADHD/ODD symptoms. This was confirmed by observations of more disruptive behavior in the classroom and at lunch, by more off-task behavior in the classroom, and by less positive engagement in classroom activities. In addition, boys reported lower friendship quality and they endorsed more hostile instrumental solutions to social problems than did girls. Finally, they were rated as more "asocial" than girls and as showing more relational aggression. Girls were rated higher than boys on mother–child conflict. Despite, these gender differences, there were no gender by trajectory interactions. Thus, gender differences are not discussed further.

SUMMARY AND CONCLUSIONS

In summary, trajectory groups were compared on measures of academic and cognitive functioning, teacher reports of behavior problems and social competence, self-reports of peer relationships, friendships, and hostile attribution biases, observations of behavior in school, and maternal reports of discipline and mother–child conflict. The two high-aggression groups differed from the two low-aggression groups on most outcome measures indicating that their aggression trajectories were associated with a

84

variety of negative outcomes at third grade reflecting poorer academic performance, lower social competence with teachers and peers, and less behavioral control in the classroom, as well as more mother–child conflict.

At the same time, there were substantial differences between the two relatively more aggressive trajectory groups that included cognitive and academic functioning, social competence, hostile attributional biases, and more conflict with mothers, teachers, and peers. This suggests that the children in these groups differ in the pattern of their problems rather than merely in the severity of problem behavior, with the moderate aggression group showing fewer signs of hostile and dysregulated aggression than those in the high-aggression trajectory group.

In contrast, the two low groups did not differ from the moderate and sharply declining group on most measures. This illustrates that the children who showed a moderate amount of mother-rated aggression at 24 and 36 months and whose aggression had declined to a low level by 54 months performed like children low in aggression at 24 and 36 months across this broad set of third grade measures. This is consistent with the interpretation that these children were showing only age-related aggression associated with early autonomy and the development of self-regulation.

Of particular interest are the contrasts between the two moderate aggression groups who started out with similar levels of aggressive behavior at 24 months, but then diverged over the course of development. These two groups differed on only a few 3rd grade measures, suggesting more mother–child conflict and modestly higher levels of disruptive behavior in third grade among those on the moderate and only slightly declining aggression trajectory. Comparisons on earlier measures suggested that early differences in self-regulatory skills may partly explain these diverging patterns of aggression in the preschool years. Overall, the follow-up analyses suggested that children in the moderate aggression group were more poorly regulated than children in the steeply declining group, but they were also less hostile and aggressive than children in the highest trajectory group.

VI. VARIABLE- AND PERSON-CENTERED ANALYSES OF PHYSICAL AGGRESSION COMPARED

In this chapter we contrast the variable- and person-centered approaches to analyzing these data. We report a hierarchical linear model (HLM) analysis of the aggression scores from 24 months to third grade, and contrast this approach with the person-centered analyses described in the previous chapters.

The two approaches are both conducted at the same level of analysis, which is at the level of the person. Both focus on describing individual differences. The variable-centered approach, however, assumes a single population and estimates a mean growth curve for that population. The population growth curve, called the unconditional model, is described by two coefficients, an estimated intercept (mean level of aggression) and an estimated slope (rate of change in aggression over all the assessments). Significant variability around these parameters means that children vary significantly in their individual growth curves, and additional modeling can determine whether differences in predictors of interest relate to individual deviations from the group growth curve.

As discussed in Chapter III, the person-centered approach begins similarly with individual growth curves modeled with random coefficients estimated as continuous latent growth factors, i.e., intercepts and slopes. This method then tests whether individual differences are a result of the presence of discrete populations, or trajectory classes, each with its estimated means and variances on the longitudinal variable of interest. The method seeks to identify the populations or classes empirically and estimates prototypic patterns of development for each population. Classification of individuals is based on estimated posterior probabilities that indicate the likelihood of a particular case belonging to each trajectory class. Each class is characterized by a specific developmental trajectory, and individuals within trajectory classes are assumed to show trivial differences from one another. In effect, all individuals in a trajectory group are characterized by the same growth curve parameters. Predictors of patterns of change are identified by asking whether individual differences in predictors differentiate trajectory groups. Thus, the two approaches answer somewhat different questions about developmental trajectories (Burchinal & Appelbaum, 1991), and provide differential power to identify potential antecedents and consequences of early aggression.

Hierarchical linear models (Bryk & Raudenbush, 2002; Singer & Willett, 2003) were used to estimate individual growth curves and identify child, family, and child-care predictors of individual developmental patterns. This approach easily accommodates information from multiple levels of nesting in the data such as repeated measures of child and family characteristics. Individual and group growth curves are estimated simultaneously to describe developmental trajectories or patterns of change over time. The individual growth curves can be predicted from both between-subjects factors such as gender and time-varying factors such as demographic and parenting factors. HLM can accommodate missing values, and variations in the timing of data collection. It also allows for flexible specification of the within-subject and between-subjects variance.

UNCONDITIONAL INDIVIDUAL AND GROUP GROWTH CURVES

We estimated individual and group quadratic growth curves using an HLM approach in a manner that as closely as possible paralleled the person-centered analysis. The HLM and trajectory analyses involved specifying the same distribution for the longitudinal measures, using the same order for the growth curve model. The analyses, of course, differed on how the growth curves were estimated. Then we related the estimated developmental functions to the same sets of child and family predictors and third grade child outcomes, looking at the same three issues. First, we sought to identify antecedents related to differences in individual growth curves, whereas in the person-centered analyses we sought to identify antecedents related to membership in individual trajectory groups. We examined the same demographic, family, child, and child-care characteristics that preceded or were collected at the same time as the mother's first rating of aggression to identify factors that were associated with individual growth curves. Second, we asked whether changes over time on the same demographic, family, child, and child-care characteristics that were collected concurrently with the maternal aggression ratings accounted for differences in individual growth curves. Finally, we asked whether the same set of developmental outcomes in third grade were related to individual aggression growth curves.

The marked skew in the aggression scores prevented us from using the typical HLM approach based on general linear models. The skew was due to

TABLE 14

GROUP GROWTH CURVE PARAMETER ESTIMATES[a]

	Model 1	Model 2
Fixed effects		
Group GC parameters	B (SE)	B (SE)
Intercept (predicted mean at 2 years)	.566***	.383***
	(.014)	(.011)
Linear	−.364***	
Age slope	(.017)	
Quadratic age	−.007**	−.077***
Slope	(.003)	(.001)
Scale adjustment	.455	.542

[a]Model estimated using log-transformed aggression data.
**$p < .01$.
***$p < .001$.

the large number of children rated as having no aggression at each age. The typical HLM approach assumes that the longitudinal outcome variable has an approximately normal distribution, but there are no transformations that can change the highly skewed aggression scores into normally distributed outcomes. Instead, the distribution of this variable falls into a Poisson distribution. The Poisson distribution describes count data, and our aggression scores are a weighted count of the number of aggressive behaviors endorsed by mothers. The person-centered trajectory analysis also assumed a Poisson distribution for the underlying data.

The unconditional individual and group growth curves were estimated using this nonlinear HLM. The model analyzes the log of the number of mother-reported aggressive behaviors so all estimated parameters and variances are in a log scale. Age was centered at 24 months so the intercept represents the estimated log-transformed aggression level at 24 months. Two quadratic models were examined—a model with estimated individual intercepts, linear, and quadratic age slopes and a model with only the intercept and quadratic age slope.

Table 14 shows the results from fitting both models. The model with only the intercept and quadratic age slope seemed to fit the data better (see Figure 4), and high correlations between estimated intercepts and linear slopes ($r = .9$) led us to select this model for all subsequent analyses. The overall fit of the two models was tested with a chi-square. Both models fit the data well. The model with the random-effects intercepts and quadratic slopes ($\chi^2_{(df = 3, \; n = 1194)}) = 3196$, $p < .001$) provided a better fit to the data, however, than did the model with the random-effects intercepts, linear slopes, and quadratic slopes ($\chi^2_{(df = 6, \; n = 1194)}) = 3156$, $p < .001$.

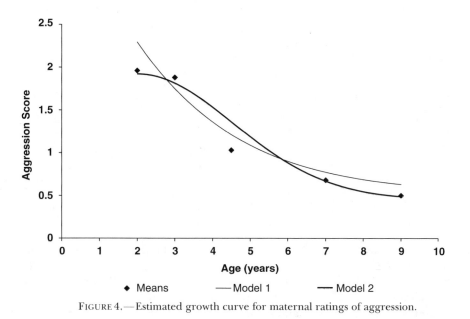

FIGURE 4.—Estimated growth curve for maternal ratings of aggression.

Overall, children showed relatively low levels of aggressive behaviors at the average age of 24 months as indicated by the estimated intercept (in log scale: $B = .383$, $SE = .011$; transformed back to original scale: $B = 1.99$). They showed marked declines in number and severity of aggressive behaviors, showing faster declines during early childhood than during the middle childhood years. The negative quadratic linear slope (in log scale: $B = -.007$, $SE = .001$) describes this marked decline in the number of aggressive behaviors during early childhood and a slower decline during middle childhood. Both estimated group growth curves shown in Figure 4 illustrate this pattern of decline and leveling off. Finally, as can be seen from the estimated variances in Table 15, there are substantial individual differences in individual intercepts and quadratic age slopes, and a high correlation between intercept and slope ($r = .78$).

Next, the estimated growth curves from the HLM and the trajectory analyses were compared by testing the extent to which there were trajectory group differences in individual growth curve parameters. Results are shown in Table 16 and Figure 5. Not surprisingly, the trajectory groups showed marked differences in mean individual growth curve parameters. The five trajectory groups account for 71–74% of the variance in the estimated individual intercepts and slopes. This analysis indicated good agreement between trajectory group characterizations and individual growth curve parameters for all five trajectory groups, as can be seen by comparing the trajectory group growth curves in Figure 1 with the mean

TABLE 15

RANDOM VARIANCE–COVARIANCE ESTIMATES[a]

	Model 1			Model 2	
	Intercept	Linear	Quadratic	Intercept	Quadratic
Intercept	.652***	.215***	−.017***	.741***	.025***
	(.014)	(.015)	(.002)	(.010)	(.001)
Linear		.155***	.011***		
Age slope		(.010)	(.002)		
Quadratic			.003***		.044***
Age slope			(.010)		(.001)

[a]Model estimated for log-transformed aggression data.
***$p < .001$.

individual growth curves by trajectory group in Figure 5. Children in the "low" trajectory group had, on average, lower levels of aggression at 24 months and showed moderate levels of decline over time. Children on the "moderate and steeply declining" trajectory had, on average, moderate levels of aggression at 24 months and showed marked declines over time. Children on the moderate, slightly declining and high trajectories had, on average, moderate or high initial levels, respectively, and little change over time. In contrast, there seemed to be a discrepancy between the two analyses with regard to the amount of change over time in the first trajectory group, labeled very low in the trajectory analysis. Although the average slope coefficient for this group had the largest negative value in the HLM analysis and appeared to show only modest change in the trajectory analysis, the actual amount of decline for this group in the HLM analysis was less than the slope coefficient implied. This is because the intercept (predicted value at 24 months) was also closest to zero. Therefore, this group had less opportunity to show large changes since it started at 24 months with the lowest values and the group growth curve approached zero more quickly. As shown in Figure 5, this group declined to a predicted value very close to zero and remained there.

INDIVIDUAL GROWTH CURVE ANALYSIS AND ANTECEDENT PREDICTORS

The next set of analyses identified demographic, family, child, and child-care experiences during the child's first 2 years of life that predicted the individual aggression growth curve parameters, intercept, and slope. These analyses began with a multivariate test that asked whether a given predictor was related to the two aggression growth curve parameters. When this multivariate test was significant, we examined the univariate associations. These analyses were conducted twice. The first analysis examined each

TABLE 16

CORRESPONDENCE BETWEEN HLM AND TRAJECTORY INDICES OF AGGRESSION

	Model Fit R^2	Trajectory Group Growth Curve Estimates				
		Group 1 Very Low	Group 2 Low	Group 3 Moderate/Decline	Group 4 Moderate	Group 5 High
N		547	302	131	184	30
Individual	.74*** B (SE)	−.109	.407	.944	1.121	1.614
Intercept		(.325)	(.313)	(.285)	(.236)	(.235)
Individual	.71*** B (SE)	−.105	−.063	−.080	−.029	−.004
Quadratic slope		(.012)	(.029)	(.012)	(.020)	(.011)

*** $p < .001$.

characteristic individually without any covariates, and the second analysis added as covariates child gender, maternal education, ethnicity, 6–24 month income/needs ratio (log transformed), and whether the child had two parents in the household in infancy. Results showing the zero-order associations are shown on the left side of Table 17 and those showing the association after adjusting for gender and the demographic characteristics are shown on the right side of Table 17. These results can be compared with results presented in Table 8. Each row presents results from a separate analysis, and the coefficients relating that predictor to the estimated individual intercept and slope

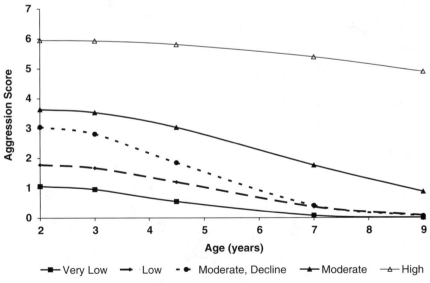

FIGURE 5.—Estimated growth curves of aggression by trajectory group.

TABLE 17

CHILD, FAMILY, AND CHILD-CARE CHARACTERISTICS FROM 1–24 MONTHS AS PREDICTORS OF AGGRESSION INTERCEPT AND SLOPE

	Model Without Covariates			Model With Covariates		
		Individual Aggression Growth Curve Parameters			Individual Aggression Growth Curve Parameters	
		Intercept	Quadratic Age Slope		Intercept	Quadratic Age Slope
	Multivariate Test	Effect size	Effect Size	Multivariate Test	Effect Size	Effect Size
	$F_{(2,1138)}$			$F_{(2,1138)}$		
Sociodemographics						
Income/needs	29.0***	−.22***	−.19***	6.7***	−.15***	−.11**
Maternal Education	23.1***	−.18***	−.19***	5.7**	−.08*	−.12***
Partner in household	8.5***	−.12***	−.10***	0.1	−.01	−.02
Race: (white = 1)	6.8**	−.11***	−.07*	1.3	−.04	−.009
Child characteristics						
Male	11.2***	.14***	.10***	10.4***	.13***	.10**
Child cognition	22.0***	−.19***	−.18***	3.1*	−.08*	−.08*
Family/maternal characteristics						
Maternal sensitivity	20.9***	−.18***	−.17***	2.2	−.07	−.06
HOME environment	27.7***	−.21***	−.19***	5.27**	−.12**	−.11**
Childrearing Attitudes	20.1***	.16***	.18***	4.63**	.05	.10***
Maternal depression	75.7***	.36***	.29***	52.7***	.32***	.26***
Child care						
Child-care quality	6.9**	−.13***	−.09***	2.9	−.09	−.06
Total hours of care		−.06	.002	3.7*	−.02**	.001
Center care		−.02	−.03	.8	−.02	−.04
Risk index						
Cumulative risk 1–24 months	42.3***	.27***	.23***			

*p < .05.
**p < .01.
***p < .001.

are in the last two columns. Effect sizes were computed to show the anticipated standardized change in the individual growth curve parameters associated with a 1 SD change in the predictor, and were computed as: $d = B\sigma_X/\sigma_Y$.

Analyses that related demographic, family and child character and child-care experiences in the child's first 2 years of life to trajectory group or to the individual growth curve parameters yielded similar conclusions. Each of the selected sociodemographic, child, and family characteristics as well as the overall risk index was related to both the individual aggression growth curve intercept and slope. In terms of the effects of child-care characteristics, only quality of care was associated with the intercept and slope of aggression in the model without covariates. As with the trajectory analysis, children with higher overall levels of aggression differed on all these selected characteristics and had higher social risk scores in general. All of the characteristics were also related to patterns of change over time in aggression ratings. Children showed lower levels of aggression and steeper declines in aggressive be-haviors when their families (in the child's first 2 years) had more income, mothers had more education and a partner, the child was white, mothers were more sensitive in interactions with their infants and home environments were more responsive and stimulating, and, when children attended child care of higher quality during the first two years of life. Higher levels of cognitive functioning also predicted lower levels and faster declines in aggression. In contrast, boys and children with more social risk factors had higher initial levels of aggressive behavior and slower declines in aggression over time. In addition to the overall risk index, more traditional childrearing attitudes and higher levels of maternal depressive symptoms predicted higher levels and slower declines in aggression. All effect sizes were small to moderate.

Next, we tested the extent to which the selected child, family, and child-care characteristics predicted individual aggression growth curve parameters after adjusting for gender and family demographics. Results are shown on the right side of Table 17. When child-care characteristics were tested, other child-care measures were also controlled. Significant predictors included two demographic indicators, maternal education and family income; both child characteristics, gender and cognitive skills; three of four family characteristics: stimulation in family environment, childrearing attitudes, and maternal depression; and one child-care characteristic: average hours/week in child care. Again, effect sizes tended to be small, with maternal depressive symptoms in the first two years being the only predictor showing a moderate association with aggression.

INDIVIDUAL GROWTH CURVES AND CONCURRENT PREDICTORS

The second set of analyses asked whether change over time in individual growth curves was related to patterns of change in concurrent child, family, and child-care characteristics. Again, we looked at each predictor in separate analyses, but in these analyses the outcome was the repeated assessment of the child, family, or child-care characteristic and the predictors in the model were the individual aggression growth curve parameters. The analyses included a block test of the two parameters. The block test was applied to the main effects that tested whether the growth curve parameters were related to the overall level of the selected characteristic and to the interaction with age that tested whether the growth curve parameters were related to linear changes over time in the selected characteristics. The analyses were conducted with and without the demographic and gender covariates. Effect sizes were computed as above for the continuously measured characteristics ($d = B\sigma_X/\sigma_Y$) and as standardized logistic regression coefficients for the categorically measured characteristics. Results are shown in Table 18 and can be compared with the results in Table 11.

These analyses yielded results similar to the analyses in which aggression trajectory groups were compared on the repeated measures of the characteristics. Children with lower levels of aggressive behavior, on average over time (from 24 months to third grade), lived in families with higher incomes, lower levels of maternal depression, and higher levels of maternal sensitivity and stimulation in the home; they were more likely to have a father in the household, to have higher cognitive scores, and to spend more hours per week in child care. However, only two variables were significant when we asked whether *changes* in the predictor variables were associated with *changes* in aggression: family income and stimulation in the home environment. When stimulation and family income increased, aggression declined more rapidly. The pattern of results was very similar when gender and demographic variables were entered as covariates. In these analyses, only the changes in income were related to the individual aggression growth curve parameters. As can be seen in the right-hand column of Table 18, when family income increased, aggression declined more rapidly. Because delay of gratification and impulsive responses on the CPT were found to differentiate between those on moderate and steeply declining and moderate and stable trajectories (see Chapter V), we also examined whether they were associated more generally with level or rate of change in aggression in the HLM analysis; neither was significant.

INDIVIDUAL GROWTH CURVES AND THIRD GRADE DEVELOPMENTAL OUTCOMES

The individual growth curve parameters were then used to predict third grade outcomes. The left columns of Table 19 show the partial correlations, correlating each parameter with each outcome adjusting for

TABLE 18

INDIVIDUAL AGGRESSION GROWTH CURVE INTERCEPTS AND SLOPES AS PREDICTORS IN LONGITUDINAL ANALYSES OF 24 MONTH TO GRADE 3 MEASURES OF FAMILY, CHILD CARE, AND CHILD CHARACTERISTICS

Predictor	Without Covariates			With Covariates		
	Block F	Intercept Effect Size d	Quadratic Slope Effect Size d	Block F	Intercept Effect Size d	Quadratic Slope Effect Size d
Sociodemographics						
Income—growth curve parameter main effect	31.8***	−.19***	−.04	9.1***	−.13**	.01
Growth curve parameter × age	4.4*	.00	−.002**	4.6*	.00	−.002**
Partner—growth curve parameter main effect[a]	20.7***	.67**	1.00	1.7		
Growth curve parameter × age	1.12	1.00	.99	.7		
Family/maternal characteristics						
Maternal sensitivity—growth curve parameter main effect	26.9***	−.09*	−.11**	7.2***	−.006	−.09
Growth curve parameter × age	.1			1.0		
HOME total—growth curve parameter main effect	54.6***	−.31***	−2.43*	22.6***	−.11**	−.07
Growth curve parameter × age	5.1**	.002*	−.06**	2.2		
Maternal depression—growth curve parameter main effect	72.7***	.26***	.07	52.0***	.24***	.04
Growth curve parameter × age	2.4			2.60	−.002	.002
Child characteristics						
Cognitive—growth curve parameter Main effect	33.3***	−.17***	−.07	8.4***	−.10*	−.03
Growth curve parameter × age	3.4*	.001*	−.00	.6		

Table 18. (Contd.)

Predictor	Without Covariates			With Covariates		
	Block F	Intercept Effect Size d	Quadratic Slope Effect Size d	Block F	Intercept Effect Size d	Quadratic Slope Effect Size d
Child-care characteristics						
Quality—growth curve parameter main effect	4.6*	−.11	−.006	1.5		
Growth curve parameter × age	1.8			.8		
Center care—growth curve parameter main effect	1.0			.33		
Growth curve parameter × age	3.4			1.73		
Total hours/week—growth curve parameter main effect	7.2***	−.17**	.13**	7.4***	−.17***	.16***
Growth curve parameter × age	2.1	.002	−.001			
Risk index—growth curve parameter main effect	47.2***	.19***	.10*	1.7	.00	−.06
Growth curve parameter × age	1.7					

*p < .05.
**p < .01.
***p < .001.
[a]Effect size for categorical variables reported as increase in odds ratio per month.

gender differences, and the results from multivariate regressions in which the individual aggression growth curve intercepts and quadratic slopes were the predictors and gender was the covariate. The high correlation between the two aggression individual growth curve parameters ($r = .78$) led us to first ask whether the two indices together were related to outcomes, and, if so, whether either the individual intercept or slope contributed when considered together along with gender. As in the trajectory analysis, omnibus tests were conducted prior to examining the regression analysis of each third grade outcome. Highly skewed outcomes were categorized as indicated in the previous chapter, and rank-order partial correlations were computed for those outcomes. Results from analyses of child outcomes in Table 19 can be compared with similar analysis reported in Table 13. Again, two sets of analyses were conducted: one analysis adjusted only for gender and a second also adjusted for demographic characteristics. In both, a block test was conducted and if significant then effect sizes for the two growth curve parameters were examined. The effect sizes were computed as $d = B\sigma_X/\sigma_Y$ for the continuous outcomes and as standardized regression coefficients for the categorical outcomes.

Analyses that included only gender as the covariate revealed a similar pattern as was observed when the outcomes were tested for trajectory group differences in Chapter V. As before, individual aggression growth curve parameters were significantly associated with each set of third grade outcomes in the omnibus tests. The univariate tests of each child outcome in the two sets of analyses also yielded similar results. Aggression trajectory groups and individual growth curve parameters were both related to academic outcomes, parenting outcomes, social competence outcomes, most school behavior problem measures, most self-reported peer relationship measures, and most teacher-reported peer relationship measures. The three observational measures of behavior in school were all significantly related to the growth curve parameters, but only one of the three showed trajectory group differences.

Interpretation of the results from the analyses using the growth curve parameters was complicated by the high correlation between estimated intercepts and slopes from individual growth curves. The high correlation meant that both indices were correlated with the outcomes when considered alone, but when they were considered together either only the individual slope parameter or neither parameter contributed. In comparison, the follow-up contrasts in analyses involving the trajectory groups were easier to interpret.

The final set of analyses added demographic variables to control for concurrent family characteristics: child ethnicity, maternal education, whether the mother was partnered in third grade, and family income-to-needs ratio at third grade. Conclusions about associations between the

97

TABLE 19

INDIVIDUAL AGGRESSION GROWTH CURVE PARAMETERS AS PREDICTORS OF THIRD GRADE OUTCOMES

	Correlations		Model With Gender as Only Covariate			Model With Gender and Demographic Characteristics as Covariates		
	Intercept r	Quadratic Age Slope r	Block $F_{(2,1138)}$	Intercept d	Quadratic Age Slope d	Block $F_{(2,1138)}$	Intercept d	Quadratic Age Slope d
Academic outcomes			11.2***			1.9		
Cognitive	−.18***	−.19***	20.4***	−.09	−.12*			
Achievement	−.18***	−.19***	19.1***	−.09	−.12*			
Parenting—mother report			79.0***			71.2***		
Harsh discipline	.16***	.17***	15.2***	.07	.12*	3.9*	.01	.08
Mother–child conflict	.42***	.46***	147.7***	.18***	.40***	146.9***	.21***	.40***
Social competence at school			15.9***			8.5***		
Social skills	−.23***	−.24***	32.2***	−.11*	−.17**	17.2***	−.07	−.14**
Teacher–child closeness	−.14***	−.15***	7.2***	−.05	−.08	4.3*	−.02	−.08
Observed behavior in school			6.6***			4.0***		
Off-task	.10**	.14***	8.6***	−.04	.17**	6.6***	−.06	.16**
Positive involvement in class	−.18***	−.18***	12.8***	−.08	−.11	5.2**	−.06	−.07
Positive with peers at lunch	−.10**	−.06	5.5**	−.14**	.04	3.7*	−.14*	.06

Table 19. (Contd.)

	Correlations		Model With Gender as Only Covariate			Model With Gender and Demographic Characteristics as Covariates		
	Intercept r	Quadratic Age Slope r	Block $\chi^2_{(2)}$	Intercept b	Quadratic Age Slope b	Block $\chi^2_{(2)}$	Intercept b	Quadratic Age Slope b
Behavior problems at school								
School performance[a]	.21***	.21***	46.6***	.15*	.14*	28.8***	.08	.10
Externalizing[a]	.21***	.24***	45.9***	.12	.23***	12.9**	.08	.22**
Internalizing[a]	.11***	.12	54.1***	.06	.11	34.4***	.03	.10
ADHD/ODD[a]	.18***	.20***	14.0***	.09	.20**	7.5*	.06	.16*
Teacher–child conflict[a]	.19***	.20***	30.6***	.14	.17*	14.8***	-.09	.14
Observed disruptive at lunch[a]	.09	.12*	33.4***			15.6***		
Observed disruptive in class[a]	.06**	.08***	10.7**	-.04	.16*	1.9		
Teacher report of peer relationships								
Asocial[a]	.08*	.06	3.8			4.4		
Excluded[a]	.16***	.17***	24.6***	.11	.13*	24.7***	.07	.09
Victimized[a]	.17***	.21***	27.0***	.02	.23***	23.8***	.0	.20***
Relational aggression[a]	.14***	.18***	40.2***	.04	.23***	24.1***	.0	.23***
More than 2 friends[a]	.13***	.12***	15.4***	.09	.06	5.6*	.08	.04
Self-reports of peer relationships								
Loneliness[a]	.16***	.15***	29.0***	.18*	.08	9.2**	.08	.08
Friendship quality	-.02	.02	1.4			.6		
Victimization[a]	.12***	.15***	23.2***	.04	.21**	15.1***	.03	.19*
Bully[a]	.22***	.25***	32.9***	.11	.24**	29.8***	.08	.26**
Hostile instrumental[a]	.04*	.06	2.8			1.0		
Hostile relational[a]	.07*	.08*	6.4*	.05	.17	2.9		

*p < .05.
**p < .01.
***p < .001.
[a]Categorical child outcome.

individual aggression growth curve parameters and outcomes in third grade were almost unchanged when these covariates were added, whereas many of the significant trajectory group differences were reduced to non-significance when the covariates were controlled. As with the trajectory analyses, gender by aggression interactions were examined; only one out of 27 tests was significant, so no follow-up tests were conducted.

COMPARISON OF FINDINGS FROM THE VARIABLE-CENTERED HLM AND PERSON-CENTERED TRAJECTORY ANALYSES

Similar conclusions regarding antecedents, concurrent covariates, and third grade outcomes were drawn from both sets of analyses. Although the HLM approach provided greater power to detect associations, the trajectory approach provided face-valid descriptions of developmental patterns and results that were easier to interpret. The Poisson growth curve provided a good description of individual patterns of change over time in maternal ratings of aggressive behaviors. However, the individual growth curve parameters were highly correlated, making it difficult to determine whether family, child, and child-care characteristics and child outcomes were more strongly related to the overall level of aggression or to rates of change in aggression. This problem was due to the highly skewed nature of maternal ratings of aggression. In contrast, the person-centered analysis produced interesting classifications of children and a grouping variable that was easier to interpret. Although both analyses indicate that aggression generally declines with age, the trajectory analysis isolated groups of children showing different patterns of change, and one group showing a marked decline in aggression, differentiating this group from the other more stable trajectory groups. This group showing a sharp decline from moderate aggression in toddlerhood to low aggression in the preschool period would not have been identified in the HLM analysis that examined level and change in aggression over time as separate dimensions.

In addition, the patterns of differences in predictors and outcomes, evident in the trajectory analyses, suggest that the distinct levels and patterns of change in aggression have different implications for understanding pathways from early behavior and family context to later adjustment. For example, both analyses reveal that family risk index, maternal depressive symptoms, and the home environment are related to longitudinal patterns of aggression. Although the HLM indicates that higher risk, more depressive symptoms, and a less stimulating home environment are all related to higher levels and slower declines in aggression for the sample as a whole, the trajectory analysis provides more specific findings by allowing the comparison of trajectory group differences on these indices of risk. For example, the trajectory analysis reveals that the moderate- and high-aggression trajectory groups differ from one another not only in the overall risk index, but also in stimulation in the home, whereas the two moderate-aggression trajectory groups (slightly and steeply declining) do not differ from one another on these measures. Different sets of predictors and correlates of these aggression trajectories in turn may have implications for understanding developmental process. For example, family risk appears to be a strong correlate of the high- and stable-aggression trajectory, whereas poor regulation appears to be important in understanding the emergence of moderate and fairly stable aggression, but with less overall family risk evident. This degree of specificity was obscured in the HLM analysis.

Likewise, in terms of outcomes, the HLM analysis identified more significant correlates of aggression level and change in aggression in the sample as a whole, but not the specific patterns of outcome that varied by trajectory group. Most important, the group showing a marked decline in aggression by school entry and generally good adjustment by third grade was identified only in the trajectory analysis, and the differences in the patterns of problems shown by the moderate stable- and high stable-aggression trajectory groups were also not evident. These issues will be addressed further in the discussion.

VII. DISCUSSION

The research presented in this *Monograph* describes the course of physical aggression in children from 24 months to third grade. Using a person-centered approach, maternal ratings of aggression were used to assign children to five specific aggression trajectory groups that reflected distinct underlying patterns of aggressive behavior over time. Early (1–24 months) predictors and longitudinal correlates of aggression trajectories were also examined. The five trajectory groups were then compared on a range of third grade outcomes. We entertained specific explanatory hypotheses about children on different aggression trajectories, and also examined how well individual risk factors and a general risk index accounted for membership in the aggression trajectory groups. Finally, we compared the findings from the trajectory analysis with a variable-centered HLM analysis and reviewed the relative costs and benefits of the person- and variable-centered approaches for describing the course of early physical aggression.

THE COURSE OF EARLY PHYSICAL AGGRESSION

Items from the CBCL were selected to index-specific features of physical aggression toward people, animals, and objects that could be measured longitudinally to track changes in aggression over time. Consistent with other research on the developmental course of aggression (Hartup, 1974; Tremblay, 2000), mothers rated most children as showing relatively low levels of physical aggression at 24 months and the mean levels of aggression generally declined from 24 months ($M = 1.96$) to third grade ($M = .50$). Moreover, particular aggressive behaviors were more common than others, even at 24 months. For example, roughly 30% of children were rated as sometimes or often destructive of their own or others' belongings at 24 and 36 months, but only about 14% were seen as ever "cruel to animals" or ever likely to "attack" people in toddlerhood. By first grade, the ratings on these items had dropped substantially to 15% for sometimes or often destructive and 4% for sometimes cruel to animals. These ratings underscore the fact that even though aggression is normative in early childhood, the type of aggression that mothers report is primarily aggression toward siblings and peers. In the current sample, this is reflected in the relatively high proportion of children rated as sometimes or often likely to hit or bully others: slightly over 70% at 24 and 36 months. However, the drop between 36 and 54 months on this item was dramatic. By 54 months, only about 20% of children were rated as sometimes or often hitting others and by third grade this had dropped to only 12%. Thus, in general, children show relatively low levels of physically aggressive behavior and even these behaviors decline dramatically between 36 and 54 months, presumably as children develop more sophisticated language and emotion regulation skills that are reflected in more socially appropriate strategies to resolve disputes with others (Calkins, 1994; Hartup, Laursen, Stewart, & Eastenson, 1988; Shantz, 1987; Tremblay, 2000). The development of effortful control over impulses is also likely to play a role in the decline of aggression as children become better at regulating not only emotion but also behavior (Eisenberg & Fabes, 1998; Kochanska, 1995; Kopp, 1989). Thus, quite low levels of physical aggression were in evidence in this normative sample by the time children were in third grade.

The descriptive data presented on aggression trajectories in Chapter III and the variable-centered HLM analysis of growth curves presented in Chapter VI both confirm the general decline in maternal ratings of physical aggression as children develop, with a notable drop in aggressive behavior in early childhood. Examination of the five aggression trajectories and the high correlation between intercept and slope in the HLM analysis indicates that most children who were more aggressive at 24 months were likely to remain more aggressive relative to peers, even as normative levels of aggression declined. Further, children who did not show early aggression were not likely to become aggressive over time according to maternal reports.

Although there was general concordance between these two analytic approaches, with both demonstrating overall declines in physical aggression as perceived by mothers, the person-centered analysis also provided a clearer picture of distinct, and potentially informative, longitudinal patterns of aggression. Of particular interest was the finding that although most children (70%) were in the two low-aggression trajectory groups (very low or low), the other three groups, which constituted 30% of the sample, showed modest to high levels of physical aggression at some point over the period between 24 months and third grade. One group showed moderate aggression at 24 and 36 months, but then a rapid decline to almost no aggression by first grade (12%) in contrast to 15% of the sample with at least moderate and continuing levels of aggression over the course of the study.

103

In fact, the rapidly declining group showed slightly more aggression at 24 months than the group with moderate early aggression that subsequently declined only slightly. These two contrasting trajectories of aggressive behavior were not identified in the variable-centered HLM analysis, which demonstrated an overall decline in aggressive behavior in early childhood rather than different patterns of decline.

In addition, consistent with other studies examining person-centered trajectories of aggressive behavior, we identified a small subset of children (3%) with a relatively high and stable aggression trajectory. Our findings are in accord with others (e.g., Broidy et al., 2003; Nagin & Tremblay, 1999) who have used a person-centered methodology to trace trajectories of physical aggression from kindergarten to early adolescence in that we also identified subgroups of children on low, moderate, and high physical aggression trajectories. Unique to our study is the trajectory group showing moderate aggression in toddlerhood that then declines to normative levels by school entry, underscoring the age-related nature of aggression in some very young children.

The only other study to examine trajectories of aggressive behavior in children from toddlerhood to middle childhood (Shaw et al., 2003) focused on low-income boys and included CBCL items tapping both physical aggression and noncompliance, a variable that they called "overt antisocial behavior." Shaw et al. (2003) identified four trajectories, but not a group showing a sharp decline in aggression between 36 and 54 months. Possibly because Shaw and colleagues also included items assessing more normative noncompliance (disobedience, temper tantrums), examined a group at somewhat higher risk for problem behavior, and only included boys, a much larger proportion of children (80%) were in moderate to high declining groups and only 14% were considered consistently low in aggression and noncompliance by their mothers. In addition, 6% of Shaw's sample was in the high and persistently "antisocial" group. Shaw et al. (2003) also noted that boys in their sample became less aggressive and noncompliant over time, even though some children remained relatively more antisocial than their peers, and in general they reported higher levels of aggression overall than we do, likely reflecting differences in sample composition and the items making up the measure of aggressive behavior.

Neither our study nor Shaw's identified a group showing emerging aggression at school entry or by third grade according to mother reports. This is important because there have been speculations about the age of onset of serious aggression as well as about how early "early starting" aggressive and antisocial behavior may be expected to emerge (American Psychiatric Association, 1994; Campbell et al., 2000; Greenberg, Speltz, & DeKlyen, 1993; Moffitt, 1993; Patterson et al., 1989; Shaw et al., 2000), ranging from the early preschool period to middle childhood. Our findings are consistent with those who argue that it is possible to identify a small group of high-risk children who are persistently aggressive as early as the preschool period (Campbell et al., 2000; Moffitt et al., 1996; Patterson et al., 1989; Shaw et al., 2000), although it is also important to emphasize the fact that not all children in our sample who showed some early aggression remained aggressive. Bennett, Lipman, Racine, and Offord (1998) have also pointed out the hazards of assuming that all early aggression may be clinically significant and they argue that not all young aggressive children are on a high-risk pathway. In addition, studies of school-age children (Broidy et al., 2003) suggest that some boys increase their levels of aggression from middle childhood to adolescence, but it is important to note that these tend to be the children in the highest aggression groups initially, representing an escalation of aggression rather than newly emerging aggression and the ratings in these studies are obtained from teachers who may be more aware of aggression by middle childhood. The task, however, is not only to identify children who are at risk for stable or escalating aggression but also to understand the processes that may account for declines in aggression among children who are elevated in early childhood.

Predictors and Correlates of Mother-Rated Aggression Trajectories

Early Family Predictors of Aggression Trajectories

In addition to describing patterns of aggression over time, we asked to what degree sociodemographic, family, child, and child-care measures obtained during infancy predicted trajectory membership. We examined individual predictors and a risk index, and also specific a priori contrasts between trajectory groups of interest. In general, there were linear relationships between sociodemographic and family risk variables and children's aggression trajectory membership. In terms of individual risk indicators, those on the lowest aggression trajectories had the lowest sociodemographic risk, as reflected in higher family income and maternal education; those on the high and stable aggression trajectories lived in families with the most sociodemographic risk including lower income and maternal education. Ethnicity was confounded with these variables and was not a consistent predictor of trajectory membership. Boys were more likely than girls to be on the trajectories showing modest to high levels of early aggression.

Observational measures of maternal parenting (sensitivity, HOME) and maternal reports of childrearing attitudes and depressive symptoms also predicted trajectory membership, with lower sensitivity and stimulation, less child-centered attitudes, and more depressive symptoms associated

105

with being on a higher aggression trajectory. With demographic covariates controlled, the HOME and maternal depression scores continued to differentiate higher from lower aggression trajectory groups. The HLM analysis identified the same individual risk variables as significant predictors of aggression intercept and slope, implicating higher levels of risk with higher levels of aggressive behavior initially, and slower declines in aggression over time. With covariates controlled, more traditional attitudes toward childrearing were also associated with higher levels and less decline in aggression. Individual risk factors or their converse, promotive factors, predicted both trajectory membership and changes in aggression in the HLM analyses.

The trajectory groups also differed from one another on the overall risk index with the low-aggression trajectory group averaging 2.13 risk factors at 24 months and the high and stable trajectory group averaging 5.14. It is also important to note that, in general, children in the high trajectory group not only experienced a greater absolute number of risks but they also tended to score at more extreme levels on many indicators of family risk. When the risk index was considered in lieu of individual risk factors, the two lower aggression trajectories differed from the three trajectory groups showing modest to high early aggression, as expected. Thus, early levels of risk paralleled early levels of aggression. The cumulative risk index also predicted higher initial aggression and a slower decline in aggression in the HLM analysis. These two approaches to examining risk, consideration of individual risk indices and of an overall risk index, provided complementary information. Further, specific parenting (e.g., stimulation) and child characteristics (e.g., gender) were associated with the higher and lower trajectories of aggression in the person-centered analysis and with individual aggression growth curves in the variable-centered HLM analysis. The cumulative risk index was also a robust predictor of aggression trajectories in the person-centered analysis and of aggression growth curves in the variable-centered analysis, indicating that the absolute number of risk factors matters as well.

These findings are consistent with a large literature linking sociodemographic and family risk to more aggressive and uncontrolled behavior in young children (Borge, Rutter, Cote, & Tremblay, 2004; Campbell et al., 2000; Deater-Deckard et al., 1998; Duncan et al., 1994; Greenberg et al., 1999; Shaw et al., 1998), and conversely linking more positive proactive parenting and a more stimulating and supportive family environment to better adjustment and self-control (Belsky et al., 1996; Denham et al., 2001; Pettit et al., 2000). Research and theory indicate that supportive and involved parenting in infancy and early childhood serves a promotive function, by fostering warm and positive parent–child relationships that also scaffold children as they learn to regulate impulses and negative emotions, including those that may lead to aggression (e.g., Calkins, 1994; Denham et al., 2000; Eisenberg & Fabes, 1998; Kochanska, 1997; NICHD ECCRN, 2004; Thompson, 1998). Family adversity, as reflected in higher sociodemographic risk and more maternal depressive symptoms, is strongly associated with poorer regulatory skills and higher levels of aggression in children, and this link appears to be partially mediated by harsh parenting (e.g., CPPRG, 2002; Greenberg et al., 1993; McLoyd, 1990; Shaw et al., 2003). There is also evidence indicating that more difficult and less controlled children elicit harsher parenting (e.g., O'Connor, Deater-Deckard, Fulker, Rutter, & Plomin, 1998). The more aggressive children in our study may have elicited less engaged parenting whereas the children low in aggression may have elicited more sensitive and stimulating interaction from parents. The only other study to examine infancy measures as predictors of mother-rated aggression trajectories in young children (Shaw et al., 2003) found that observations of harsh and rejecting parenting differentiated low from high-aggression trajectory groups, also highlighting the importance of early parent–child interaction in attempting to understand different pathways of early aggressive behavior, both normative and potentially problematic.

Differential Predictors of Aggression Trajectories

So far we have considered the degree to which levels of risk and levels of aggression covary in predictable ways. However, the strength of the person-centered trajectory analysis is the identification of subgroups of children with distinct patterns of aggression over time. Therefore, of particular interest were contrasts between the two trajectory groups with moderate levels of early aggression, but different patterns of change in aggression—the moderate and steeply declining trajectory and the moderate and slightly declining trajectory (groups 3 and 4). In general, initial measures of risk did not differentiate these two trajectories and they were similar on the overall risk index (M's = 2.98), suggesting that earlier, modest levels of risk may have predicted initial moderate levels of aggression, but these family variables did not account for differences in patterns of change over time.

In contrast, when the high-aggression trajectory (group 5) was compared with the moderate, slightly declining trajectory (group 4), a number of differences in early sociodemographics, maternal parenting behavior and attitudes, and maternal depressive symptoms were evident, although they were somewhat confounded with demographics. Moreover, when the overall risk index was examined instead of correlated risk factors, these two trajectory groups showed clear differences in initial levels of risk (M's = 2.98 and 5.14). Taken together, these data make clear that initial levels of family

107

risk and initial levels of aggression were related in predictable ways, both when examining specific risk factors and the overall risk index. Children on the highest aggression trajectory experienced the highest level of family risk.

Time-Varying Family Predictors of Aggression Trajectories

We were interested not only in earlier predictors of trajectory group but also the degree to which *changes* in family characteristics and other variables were related to stability or change in patterns of aggression over time. Demographic and family measures and child cognitive functioning predicted the initial level of aggression, as already discussed, but not *changes* in aggression over time. Similarly, overall levels of family risk beyond 24 months added little to the prediction of trajectory group membership in the person-centered analyses. This may seem surprising, but it appears to reflect the relative stability of aggression (except for the moderate and steeply declining group) and of most family factors. Thus, there was inadequate variation over time to isolate factors associated with change. Although there were wide individual differences in *levels* of particular risk factors and in the overall risk index, these were relatively stable over time within families. The risk index was associated with higher levels and slower declines in aggression over time, but change in risk and change in aggression were unrelated. The fact that risk was so stable likely explains why changes in family risk could not account for the differences between the two moderately aggressive trajectory groups (steeply declining and slightly declining). These two aggression trajectories diverged between 36 and 54 months and we had hypothesized that changes in levels of family risk might be one reason for changes in levels of aggression. Although it is possible that unmeasured family variables account for these differences in aggression trajectories, within-child factors such as rate of development or temperament may also explain these differential changes in aggression.

Child-Care Measures as Predictors and Correlates of Aggression Trajectories

We also examined quality of child care, number of hours in care, and time in center care as predictors and time-varying correlates of trajectory membership. Child-care measures averaged from early infancy to 24 months were used to predict aggression trajectories. Longitudinal indicators of these same child-care predictor variables from 24 months through 54 months were also assessed. Hours in care and quality of care from infancy through 24 months showed modest relations with aggression trajectory group, but these effects were not maintained once selection effects and other child-care variables were controlled. In the longitudinal analyses, the number of hours in care between 24 and 54 months was associated with trajectory group membership even with demographic variables and child-care quality controlled. Specifically, children in the two low-aggression groups were in more hours of care between 24 and 54 months than children whose aggression was initially moderate and then declined to a low level. Children on this steeply declining aggression trajectory were also in fewer hours of care than children on the moderate and only slightly declining trajectory. Thus, when the data were examined in terms of hours in care during the period from 24 to 54 months and trajectories of mother-reported aggressive behavior were assessed using a person-centered approach, we did not find linear relations between hours in care and aggressive behavior as we did when teacher reports of aggression were examined, using a variable-centered approach to data analysis (NICHD ECCRN, 2003a). Further, the children in the most aggressive trajectory group were not in the most care in early childhood and changes in child-care hours were unrelated to trajectory group. Hours in care increased from 24 to 54 months for most children in the study, but not differentially by trajectory group. Children on the highest aggression trajectory did not experience greater increases in child-care hours than other children.

These results are not consistent with those reported in an earlier paper from this study pertaining to time spent in child care and problem behavior, including aggression (NICHD ECCRN, 2003a). In those analyses, we found that mean number of hours in care from infancy to 54 months predicted caregiver ratings of aggression at 54 months and teacher ratings of aggression in kindergarten. Hours in care were related to maternal reports of assertiveness, but not to maternal ratings of aggression. The apparent discrepancies between the current findings and our earlier report linking hours in care to children's aggression reflects our different approaches to data analysis (i.e., person-centered versus variable-centered), the fact that our measure of aggression was completed by mothers rather than caregivers and teachers, and the fact that the previous report focused on cumulative hours in child care from birth to 54 months, rather than on distinct developmental periods (3–24 months, 24–54 months) as in the current analyses. Thus, our current emphasis on subgroups of children showing different levels and patterns of aggression over time as assessed by mothers provides a different perspective on the relation between hours in care and aggressive behavior. Person-centered analyses may be especially informative when trying to explain patterns of behavior that are not common in the general population, such as steeply declining aggression or high and stable levels of aggression. However, it is also important to emphasize that children on the highest aggression trajectory were not in more hours of child care in infancy, nor did they experience greater increases in hours of care than children on other trajectories; changes in aggression also were not linked to concomitant changes in hours in child care. It is also worth noting that in the earlier work, we did not find a link between hours in care across the first 54 months of life and clinical levels of externalizing problems, although it appears that children in the highest aggression trajectory are showing quite elevated levels of problem behavior.

The HLM analysis also indicated that even when a variable-centered approach was used, fewer hours in care from infancy to 24 months predicted both higher levels of physical aggression at 24 months, and a slower decline in aggression. The children in the most child care initially were also lowest in physical aggression as rated by their mothers. Because they were already quite low in aggression, they declined only slightly due to floor effects.

Neither quality of care nor time in center care was associated systematically with aggression trajectory in the person-centered analysis or with aggression level or rate of change in aggression in the variable-centered analysis. These results also differ from our earlier report (NICHD ECCRN, 2003a), especially with regard to time in center care. In that work, we found that time spent in center care was associated with more problem behavior reported by caregivers at 54 months and by kindergarten teachers. Overall, differences in the measure, reporter, analysis strategy, and longitudinal follow-up interval (until kindergarten in the earlier report and until third grade in the current report) are likely to account for these apparent discrepancies. It should also be noted that teacher and mother agreement on levels of early aggression is not high, presumably because there is a certain amount of situational specificity to aggressive behavior in young children (e.g., NICHD ECCRN, 1998, 2001a) and because of the differential experiences of mothers and caregivers or teachers who are more likely to see many children in group settings.

Summary

Overall, then, risk factors were associated with membership in trajectory groups such that greater family risk was associated with higher and more stable aggression; conversely families low in risk or high in promotive factors had children with lower overall levels of aggression. A small group of children also showed moderate levels of aggression early on that then decreased to normative levels, but changes in family risk were not associated either predictively or longitudinally with changes in aggression from 36 months to 54 months in this group. In general, there was relative stability in both levels of aggression and levels of promotive or risk factors, and this

110

may partly account for the fact that few time-varying co-variates explained trajectory differences. Children in the steeply declining aggression group were in fewer hours of child care by 24 months than children in the low-aggression groups and those in the group showing moderate but relatively stable aggression, making interpretation of this finding difficult. One possibility is that the amount of child care is associated with more aggression only in the context of at least moderate risk and maternal depressive symptoms, consistent with the recent report by Borge et al. (2004). However, this does not explain why hours in care were unrelated to aggression in the high-aggression group, which also experienced the most risk.

Child Outcomes as a Function of Person-Centered Aggression Trajectories

Trajectory membership from 24 months to third grade was a robust predictor of outcomes at third grade as reflected in cognitive and achievement tests, teacher ratings of social competence and behavior problems, maternal reports of parenting, children's self-reports of peer experiences and hostile attributions, and observations of children's behavior in the classroom and at lunch. Outcomes were selected to minimize maternal reports as mothers' ratings were used to form trajectory groups. Thus multi-method, multi-source, and largely independent outcomes were examined.

Higher vs. Lower Aggression Trajectories

Every construct examined with controls only for gender showed main effects of trajectory group and many of the univariate follow-up analyses with planned contrasts across trajectory groups were significant. Overall, children on the two low-aggression trajectories differed from those on the two high-aggression trajectories on most outcomes, indicating that children whose mothers rated them as generally low in aggression across childhood were better adjusted, performed better academically and socially, and had better relationships with parents, teachers, and peers at third grade. Conversely, children with moderate to high levels of only *slightly declining* or *persistent* aggression, as rated by their mothers, were performing more poorly across domains (social, academic) and relationships (parents, teachers, peers); they were observed to be less engaged and more disruptive in school; and they were more likely to be rated by teachers as showing significant behavior problems. Thus, children on high or moderately stable aggression trajectories from 24 months to third grade evidenced a range of adjustment problems relative to their low-aggression trajectory counterparts. These data provide strong support for the validity of these person-centered trajectory groupings derived from maternal ratings of physical aggression.

111

Children on the two higher aggression trajectories showed similar patterns of outcomes when compared with those on the two low-aggression trajectories, but at different levels of magnitude. Differences between the highest aggression group and the lower groups were larger than were the differences between the two lower aggression groups and the moderate-aggression trajectory group. This suggests that, at a minimum, there are quantitative differences in the severity of adjustment problems between these two higher aggression trajectory groups. When these two groups were compared directly with one another children on the high-aggression trajectory also looked worse than children on the moderate-aggression trajectory. Children with the highest level of aggression from 24 months to third grade performed more poorly on academic and achievement tests, had poorer relationships with their mothers, teachers, and peers, and were less engaged in the classroom than children with moderate levels of aggression over time. Teachers rated the high-aggression trajectory children as having fewer friends at school, and the children themselves responded to hypothetical vignettes with hostile attributional biases for instrumental and relational aggression, suggesting that they are not only more aggressive themselves, but expect others to behave that way toward them. It is also important to note that many of these trajectory group differences disappeared when sociodemographic variables were controlled, suggesting that family adversity continued to account for differences across contexts at third grade.

Nevertheless, the data suggest that the children in the high-aggression trajectory group are on a pathway toward more serious and continuing antisocial behavior problems in adolescence, given their significantly higher ratings on the TRF externalizing scale as well as on specific oppositional and antisocial behaviors. By third grade, children in the high-aggression trajectory group are scoring in the at-risk range on the TRF Delinquency scale ($M = 61$) in contrast to the moderate, slightly declining group who are just above the normative level on this measure ($M = 54$). They are also more likely than children in the moderate-aggression trajectory group to meet symptom criteria for ODD (18.5% vs. 6.8%) and for a mix of ADHD and ODD symptoms at clinically elevated levels (40.7% vs. 27%). Thus, children on the high-aggression trajectory may be more akin to the stable, early starters described by others (Moffitt et al., 1996; Patterson et al., 1989) and identified in other person-centered research using teacher ratings as the basis for trajectory analysis (Broidy et al., 2003; Nagin & Tremblay, 1999). In contrast, children on the moderate-aggression trajectory may continue to experience academic and social problems, but they appear to be at lower risk for delinquency and antisocial behavior in childhood and adolescence, possibly because their difficulties reflect attentional and impulse control problems associated with reactive aggression, rather than hostile and proactive aggression associated with more serious problems in adolescence

(Coie & Dodge, 1998). Alternatively, the moderate trajectory group may show an escalating pattern of aggression by early adolescence as identified in some trajectory analyses (Broidy et al., 2003). Continued follow-up of this sample through sixth grade will allow us to address some of these questions in the future. In particular, it will be important to compare these two trajectory groups on their engagement in delinquent and risk-taking behaviors in early adolescence (e.g., drug use, vandalism, minor theft) and in terms of patterns of reactive (impulsive) and proactive (instrumental) aggression in order to determine whether qualitative differences in outcome are in evidence by sixth grade.

Early and Declining Aggression vs. Consistently Low Aggression

What are the sequelae in third grade of early appearing, but time-limited aggression? Although it was possible that the contrast between the two low-aggression trajectory groups and the moderate, but steeply declining aggression trajectory group would suggest subtle residual effects of early aggression, either in peer relations, school functioning, or mother–child relationship indices, analyses did not reveal significant between-group differences in third grade outcomes. In general, those children who had shown short-lived aggression in early childhood appeared to be functioning well within the normal range at third grade. These outcome data support the argument that these youngsters were showing age-related and normative levels of aggression and were not at risk for later difficulties. In contrast, as already noted, the children on the two more stable aggression trajectories differed from those on the two low-aggression trajectories on many measures, not only at third grade but from infancy onward. Thus, knowing a child's level of aggression in early childhood is not sufficient to predict outcomes at third grade. However, higher levels of early aggression when paired with higher levels of family adversity appear to place children at risk for more persistent problems (Campbell et al., 2000). In this data set, the moderate but declining trajectory group was relatively low in demographic and family risk, both initially and over time. These results indicate that some children with early aggression will continue on an aggressive pathway, but others will show short-lived aggression that is developmentally self-limiting, and these differences appear to be, at least in part, a reflection of the developmental context.

Diverging Trajectories of Aggression at Preschool Age

What differentiates the children on a moderate and steeply declining aggression trajectory from those whose trajectory of aggression is moderate

113

and remains relatively more stable? Why might moderate aggression be self-limiting in some children, but not others? The trajectory analysis identified groups that started out at similar moderate levels of aggression, but followed different pathways across early childhood to third grade. As discussed earlier, no risk factors clearly differentiated these groups either initially or over time, although children in the steeply declining trajectory group were in somewhat fewer hours of child care by 24 months; like other children in the sample, however, they increased their hours in care between 24 and 54 months concomitant with their decline in aggression.

By third grade, these groups differed on academic achievement, mother–child conflict, and teacher ratings of social skills and behavior problems. However, teacher and self-reports of peer relations and observations in school did not differentiate these groups. In general, those on the moderate and steeply declining trajectory performed better on the Woodcock–Johnson achievement battery, received better teacher ratings of school performance, and were seen as engaging in less conflict with their mothers, and as having fewer disruptive behavior problems than those on a moderate and more stable aggression trajectory. These group differences were, however, also associated with demographic variables at third grade.

Specific hypothesis-testing analyses were conducted to examine whether better language or self-regulatory skills in the 36–54-month period might account for differences between these two groups with moderate levels of early aggression but markedly different patterns over time, as the differences in aggression trajectory became especially marked in the preschool period. Differences were not found in language development at 36 or 54 months or in self-regulation at 36 months. However, children in the steeply declining aggression trajectory group did show better self-regulatory skills at 54 months, suggesting that their ability to regulate behavior in response to situational demands might partly explain their decrease in aggression. It is unclear to what degree these changes reflect development, temperament, or aspects of the child's environment either at home or in child care that we did not assess. Surprisingly, however, there were not many factors that unequivocally accounted for differences in these two trajectories of aggressive behavior from early to middle childhood. Future research needs to focus on the more proximal processes of family socialization of prosocial behavior and self-regulation during this age period that may be related to decreases in aggression between 36 and 54 months. In addition, experience in a group setting with caregivers and peers may help some children integrate basic social skills such as turn-taking and sharing into their repertoires; these experiences in turn may have led to better regulation of impulsive behavior and to decreases in normative, age-related aggression. Research on factors that appear to facilitate normative decreases in aggressive behavior may shed light on this issue.

114

Summary

In summary, these data suggest that elevated physical aggression at 24 months, when it occurs in the context of greater family adversity may be a marker for a stable aggression trajectory and ongoing problems in social and academic functioning, whereas modest levels of early aggression may or may not constitute a marker of continuing problems. Differences in self-regulatory skills evident by 54 months may partly account for these differing trajectories. Children who show low levels of early aggression do not appear to be at risk for emerging problems by third grade.

Person- and Variable-Centered Approaches to the Course of Physical Aggression

The comparison of person-centered and variable-centered approaches to analyzing changes in aggression as well as the analyses of the predictors, correlates, and outcomes of differing aggression trajectories show many converging findings. The variable-centered analyses indicated that most demographic, family, and child risk factors examined were associated with initial level of aggression and with changes in aggression in the expected directions. Overall, the HLM analysis identified more variables as significant predictors of aggression because this approach has more power to detect differences. This is because subgroups are not isolated in HLM analyses and individual growth curves are represented by continuous variables. Prototypic group growth curves in the person-centered analysis, on the other hand, are represented by a categorical variable. Thus, more variables are significant in HLM models even with demographic variables controlled. This gives a clearer picture of the family, child, and child-care measures associated with the emergence of aggression and with general patterns of change over time in aggression in the sample as a whole, i.e., with decreases in aggression.

At the same time, some important information is lost in the HLM analysis. The power of the person-centered approach is its ability to detect small subgroups of the larger sample that do not fit the shape of the average trajectory generated by the variable-centered approach. Further, while a variable-centered approach can identify the predictors, correlates, and outcomes of individual differences in trajectories, it cannot determine whether unique trajectory subgroups are associated with distinctive patterns of prediction and outcome. In the current analyses, this distinct contribution of person-centered analyses is illustrated by the different patterns of findings for the moderate and high-aggression subgroups. The two moderately aggressive groups with differing patterns of change in aggression through third grade were not revealed in the HLM analysis, although they are consistent with results from other studies reporting that not all children showing early disruptive behavior continue to show difficulties at school entry (Campbell, 2002). The intriguing differences between those on the highest aggression trajectory and those on the moderate-aggression trajectory also would not be identified in the HLM analyses. Only the person-centered trajectory groupings allowed us to uncover differences in hostile and aggressive behavior in these two trajectory groups. Further, the groups that started out differently in toddlerhood, but then were all rated low in aggression and were functioning well by third grade would have been overlooked in the HLM analysis. The person-centered analyses may also be especially useful for identifying differing trajectories given the high levels of skewness in the maternal ratings.

On the other hand, the variable-centered HLM provided more power to detect differences in third grade outcomes and to relate changes in aggression to outcomes in third grade. Indeed, 23 out of 27 variables assessed at third grade were related to aggression intercept and slope in the HLM with only gender controlled, and 19 variables were significant when demographic variables were also controlled. In general, consistent with expectations, better cognitive functioning and academic achievement were related to both lower initial levels of aggression and greater declines in aggression as were better peer skills as assessed by teachers and child self-reports. Conversely, teacher-reported peer problems and self-reported loneliness and victimization were associated with a higher initial level of aggression and slower declines in aggression. Observed behavior in school also was associated in the expected direction with both level of aggression and changes in aggression. Some of these hypothesized associations with level of aggression and change in aggression were not significant in the person-centered analysis because the high-aggression trajectory group was so small.

These different analyses, therefore, complement each other. The variable-centered HLM analysis identifies the many risk and promotive factors associated with higher and lower levels of aggression, as well as with meaningful changes in average aggression level over time for the sample as a whole. In contrast, the person-centered trajectory analysis provides information about distinct patterns of change in aggression among unique subgroups and the specific correlates of these varying patterns. These analyses were also easier to interpret at the process level, thereby providing information that could be used to generate follow-up hypotheses about patterns of hostility and inhibitory control that might account for differences between specific subgroups identified in the trajectory analyses. Because the person-centered analysis identified specific subgroups with different patterns of aggressive behavior over time that then predicted different levels of adjustment in middle childhood, it is an especially useful tool for longitudinal studies of individual differences. This is because problematic behavior at one point in time is likely to be less predictive than problem behavior that

persists, especially when children at risk for more serious and chronic behavior problems and school difficulties are being identified. Continued follow-up of the children in these five aggression trajectories should shed
further light on the power of this approach for identifying subgroups at
differential risk for poor outcomes in adolescence.

A Comment on Sex Differences

There has been a good deal of debate about when gender differences
in aggression emerge (e.g., Hay et al., 2000; Keenan & Shaw, 1997) and
the implications of gender differences in aggression for later adjustment
(e.g., Broidy et al., 2003). In the current report, we found that once children
were grouped into prototypic trajectories, gender by trajectory interactions
were not significant. In general, there were more girls in the two lowest aggression trajectory groups than in the three trajectory groups showing at least
moderate aggression, indicating that most girls showed only low and normative aggression. In contrast, the high and stable aggression group was 72%
male. This finding is consistent with other studies that suggest that a high
level of stable physical aggression from early to middle childhood is more
common in boys. A few girls also show aggression, and when they do, the
implications for later functioning appear to be similar (Broidy et al., 2003).

Although gender by aggression trajectory interactions were not significant when third grade outcomes were examined, gender was associated in
predictable ways with these outcomes. In general, boys were rated by their
teachers as having more peer and adjustment problems and they were
observed to be less cooperative and sociable and more disruptive at school.
In the HLM analysis, gender was likewise associated with aggression intercept and slope, such that boys were higher in aggression and they showed
a slower decline in aggressive behavior. Of particular interest would be
the small group of girls showing high levels of aggression, but even in this
large sample, only eight girls were in the high and stable aggression trajectory group, limiting the conclusions that can be drawn about this small
subgroup of aggressive girls. Clearly, this is a topic for future research.

Conclusions and Directions for Future Research

In summary, the data indicate that children on low- and high-aggression trajectories differed in expected ways from infancy to third grade. The
children on the two higher aggression trajectories experienced higher levels of family risk, including lower income, higher levels of maternal depression, and less positive caregiving in infancy and toddlerhood, and they
also functioned more poorly on early measures of cognitive functioning.
They continued to have more difficulties than their low aggressive peers in
third grade across academic and social domains, and they also exhibited

higher levels of behavior problems. In contrast, children classified in the two low-aggression trajectories experienced less family risk and more positive parenting in early childhood. Presumably partly because of their more supportive family environments and their better cognitive skills, they remained on a low-risk trajectory and were functioning well in the academic and social arenas at third grade. These results are consistent with a large body of data linking risk and promotive factors to differing developmental outcomes from early to middle childhood.

Even the two higher aggression trajectory groups showed somewhat different predictors of aggression level and different outcomes by third grade. In general, the moderately aggressive children were at lower risk than children in the high-aggression trajectory, especially with regard to early maternal depression and observed stimulation at home. At third grade, those on the high-aggression trajectory were experiencing more severe problems, including poorer academic functioning, more mother–child conflict, and more peer problems than experienced by the moderate-aggression trajectory group. The high trajectory group was more angry, hostile, antisocial, and oppositional whereas the moderate group appeared to have problems at a lower level of severity, possibly reflecting poorer self-regulatory skills.

Children who started out at different levels of aggression (low or moderate) in early childhood, and then converged to become low in aggression by school entry showed some early differences in family risk and hours in child care. Differences, however, were no longer in evidence when third grade outcomes were examined.

Children who started out as moderately aggressive in toddlerhood, but then developed along diverging trajectories, showed fewer differences than expected both early on and later. Differences in family risk over time did not appear to account for these diverging pathways, contrary to expectation. By 54 months, however, the children in the steeply declining trajectory group showed better self-regulatory skills on two laboratory measures of impulse control, suggesting that the emergence of better self-control may partly account for these differences in pathways. Unobserved family socialization practices in early childhood may also help to explain these different pathways of aggressive behavior. Only a few differences, however, were apparent between these two trajectory groups at third grade.

Continued follow-up of these children at least through sixth grade will permit us to examine how well these trajectories predict functioning in school, peer, and family contexts in early adolescence. Will the high and stable group show more antisocial and delinquent behavior than the moderate and stable group as expected? Will the three groups with low aggression by third grade continue to function well or will more age-related aggression emerge in early adolescence (Moffitt, 1993)? In addition, because conduct disorder and delinquency become more identifiable by early adolescence, we will be in a position to examine these more specific antisocial outcomes in sixth grade. Because we have measures of monitoring and supervision by parents (Patterson et al., 1989), we will also have a better sense of how age-related family processes may account for stable versus diverging trajectories in early adolescence.

Despite our robust observational measures of mother–child interaction over time, we measured only sensitive, responsive parenting and early stimulation. Our exploration of family processes would have been strengthened by observational measures of negative discipline and harsh parenting that are often associated both predictively and longitudinally with the emergence of externalizing behavior (Campbell et al., 1996; Greenberg et al., 1999; O'Connor et al., 1998; Patterson et al., 1992). In addition, a closer assessment of the strategies that parents use to support emotion and behavior regulation, especially in the preschool period, may shed light on differences in patterns of aggression over time (e.g., Calkins, 1994; Denham et al., 2000; Rubin et al., 2003). This seems especially important in view of the differences that were observed between children on the moderate and declining and moderate and stable aggression trajectories at 54 months. Finally, we did not examine bidirectional or interactive processes in mother–child interaction that might clarify why some children never became aggressive, others declined in levels of aggression, and still others stayed on aggression trajectories.

Our self-report and teacher-report measures of peer relations confirmed that children on the most aggressive pathway also had the most problems cooperating with peers and they expressed more hostile attributional biases. We did not examine earlier indicators of peer problems in this paper; hence, perhaps these peer difficulties were evident much earlier, a possibility we can explore in future analyses. Because we have observations of interactions in the laboratory with a close friend at fourth and sixth grades, we will be able to build on these findings, e.g., by assessing the degree to which trajectory differences are associated with continuing problems and problematic peer processes. For example, Dishion, Andrews, and Crosby (1995) suggest that close friends reinforce each others' antisocial behavior. We can also assess the degree to which children on more aggressive trajectories select more aggressive peers as close friends (Dishion et al., 1995; Vitaro, Brendgen, & Tremblay, 1999). As the peer group becomes more central in children's lives in pre-adolescence, it will be important to compare family and peer group influences on continuing and changing trajectories of physical aggression. Finally, because we relied on mother reports to assess aggressive behavior, we may be missing some children whose aggression is more evident at school or with peers in middle childhood, or whose aggression is evident in a more subtle form, such as relational aggression, by middle childhood.

REFERENCES

Achenbach, T. M. (1991a). *Manual for the Child Behavior Checklist/4-18 and 1991 profile*. Burlington, VT: Department of Psychiatry, University of Vermont.

Achenbach, T. M. (1991b). *Manual for the teacher's report form and 1991 profile*. Burlington, VT: Department of Psychiatry, University of Vermont.

Achenbach, T. M. (1992). *Manual for the Child Behavior Checklist/2-3 and 1992 profile*. Burlington, VT: Department of Psychiatry, University of Vermont.

Achenbach, T. M., McConaughy, S. H., & Howell, C. (1987). Child/adolescent behavioral and emotional problems: Implications of cross-information correlations for situational specificity. *Psychological Bulletin*, **101**, 213–232.

Aguilar, B., Sroufe, L. A., Egeland, B., & Carlson, E. (2000). Distinguishing the early onset/persistent and adolescence-onset/antisocial behavior types: From birth to 16 years. *Development and Psychopathology*, **12**, 109–132.

American Psychiatric Association (1994). *Diagnostic and statistical manual of mental disorders* (4th ed.). Washington, DC: Author.

Angold, A., Costello, E. J., & Erklani, A. (1999). Comorbidity. *Journal of Child Psychology and Psychiatry*, **40**, 57–87.

Asher, S. R., Hymel, S., & Renshaw, P. D. (1984). Loneliness in children. *Child Development*, **55**, 1456–1464.

Barkley, R. A. (1994). The assessment of attention in children. In G. Reid Lyon (Ed.), *Frames of reference for the assessment of learning disabilities: New views on measurement issues* (pp. 69–102). Baltimore, MD: Paul H. Brookes.

Barkley, R. A., Brodzinsky, G., & DuPaul, G. J. (1992). Frontal lobe functions in attention deficit disorder with and without hyperactivity: A review and research report. *Journal of Abnormal Child Psychology*, **20**, 163–188.

Bates, J. E., Dodge, K. A., Pettit, G. S., & Ridge, B. (1998). Interaction of temperamental resistance to control and restrictive parenting in the development of externalizing behavior. *Developmental Psychology*, **34**, 982–995.

Bayley, N. (1993). *Bayley Scales of Infant Development-II*. San Antonio, TX: Psychological Corporation.

Belsky, J. (1984). The determinants of parenting: A process model. *Child Development*, **55**, 83–96.

Belsky, J. (2001). Developmental risks (still) associated with early child care. *Journal of Child Psychology and Psychiatry*, **42**, 845–860.

Belsky, J., Hsieh, K. H., & Crnic, K. (1998). Mothering, fathering, and infant negativity as antecedents of boys' externalizing problems and inhibition at age 3 years: Differential susceptibility to rearing experience? *Development and Psychopathology*, **10**, 301–319.

Belsky, J., Woodworth, S., & Crnic, K. (1996). Troubled family interaction during toddlerhood. *Development and Psychopathology*, **8**, 477–495.

Bennett, K. J., Lipman, E. L., Racine, Y., & Offord, D. R. (1998). Do measures of externalizing behaviour in normal populations predict later outcome? Implications for targeted interventions to prevent conduct disorder. *Journal of Child Psychology and Psychiatry*, **39**, 1059–1070.

Bergman, L. R., & Magnusson, D. (1997). A person-oriented approach to research in developmental psychopathology. *Development and Psychopathology*, **9**, 291–319.

Borge, A. I. H., Rutter, M., Cote, S., & Tremblay, R. E. (2004). Early childcare and physical aggression: Differentiating social selection and social causation. *Journal of Child Psychology and Psychiatry*, **45**, 367–376.

Bracken, B. A. (1984). *Bracken Basic Concepts Scale*. San Antonio, TX: Psychological Corp.

Bradley, R. H., & Caldwell, B. M. (1984). The relation of infants' home environments to achievement test performance in first grade: A follow-up study. *Child Development*, **55**, 803–809.

Bradley, R. H., Mundfrom, D. J., Whiteside, L., Casey, P. H., & Barrett, K. (1994). A factor-analytic study of the infant–toddler and early-childhood versions of the home inventory administered to white, black, and Hispanic American parents of children born preterm. *Child Development*, **65**, 880–888.

Brame, B., Nagin, D. S., & Tremblay, R. E. (2001). Developmental trajectories of physical aggression from school entry to late adolescence. *Journal of Child Psychology and Psychiatry*, **42**, 503–512.

Broidy, L. M., Nagin, D. S., Tremblay, R. E., Bates, J. E., Brame, B., Dodge, K.A, Fergusson, D., Horwood, J. L., Loeber, R., Laird, R., Lynam, D. R., Moffitt, T. E., Pettit, G. S., & Vitaro, F. (2003). Developmental trajectories of childhood disruptive behaviors and adolescent delinquency: A six-site, cross-national study. *Developmental Psychology*, **39**, 222–245.

Bronfenbrenner, U. (1979). *The ecology of human development*. Cambridge, MA: Harvard University Press.

Brownell, C. A., & Hazen, N. (1999). Early peer interaction: A research agenda. *Early Education and Development*, **10**, 403–413.

Bryk, A. S., & Raudenbush, S. W. (2002). *Hierarchical linear models: Applications and data analysis methods* (2nd ed.). Thousand Oaks, CA: Sage.

Burchinal, M., & Appelbaum, M. (1991). Estimating individual developmental functions: Methods and their assumptions. *Child Development*, **62**, 23–43.

Burchinal, M. R., Roberts, J. E., Hooper, S., & Zeisel, S. A. (2000). Cumulative risk and early cognitive development: A comparison of statistical risk models. *Developmental Psychology*, **36**, 793–807.

Cairns, R. B., & Cairns, B. D. (1994). *Lifelines and risks: Pathways of youth in our time*. New York: Cambridge University Press.

Caldwell, B. M., & Bradley, R. H. (1984). *Home observation for the measurement of the environment*. Little Rock: University of Arkansas at Little Rock.

Calkins, S. (1994). Origins and outcomes of individual differences in emotion regulation. In N. A. Fox (Ed.), The development of emotion regulation. *Monographs of the Society for Research in Child Development*, **59** (2–3, Serial No. 240), 53–72.

Campbell, S. B. (1994). Hard-to-manage preschool boys: Externalizing behavior, social competence and family context at two-year follow-up. *Journal of Abnormal Child Psychology*, **22**, 147–166.

Campbell, S. B. (1995). Behavior problems in preschool children: A review of recent research. *Journal of Child Psychology and Psychiatry*, **36**, 113–149.

Campbell, S. B. (2002). *Behavior problems in preschool children: Clinical and developmental issues* (2nd ed.). New York: Guilford.

Campbell, S. B., Pierce, E. W., March, C. L., Ewing, L. J., & Szumowski, E. K. (1994). Hard-to-manage preschool boys: Symptomatic behavior across contexts and time. *Child Development*, **65**, 836–851.

Campbell, S. B., Pierce, E. W., Moore, G., Marakovitz, S., & Newby, K. (1996). Boys' externalizing problems at elementary school age: Pathways from early behavior problems, maternal control, and family stress. *Development and Psychopathology*, **8**, 701–720.

Campbell, S. B., Shaw, D. S., & Gilliom, M. (2000). Early externalizing behavior problems: Toddlers and preschoolers at risk for later maladjustment. *Development and Psychopathology*, **12**, 467–488.

Carnegie Council on Adolescent Development (1989). *Turning points: Preparing American youth for the 21st century, report of the task force on education of young adolescents*. New York: Carnegie Corporation.

Caron, C., & Rutter, M. (1991). Co-morbidity in child psychopathology: Concepts, issues, and research strategies. *Journal of Child Psychology and Psychiatry*, **32**, 1063–1079.

Caughy, M. O., DiPietro, J. A., & Strobino, M. (1994). Day-care participation as a protective factor in the cognitive-development of low-income children. *Child Development*, **65**, 457–471.

Cohen, J. (1988). *Statistical power analysis in the behavioral sciences* (2nd ed.). Hillsdale, NJ: Erlbaum.

Coie, J. D., & Dodge, K. A. (1998). Aggression and antisocial behavior. In N. Eisenberg (Ed.) (Editor-in-Chief: W. Damon), *Social, emotional, and personality development. Vol. 3: Handbook of child psychology* (5th ed., pp. 779–862). New York: Wiley.

Cole, P. M., Teti, L. O., & Zahn-Waxler, C. (2003). Mutual emotion regulation and the stability of conduct problems between preschool and early school age. *Development and Psychopathology*, **15**, 1–18.

Conduct Problems Prevention Research Group (1999). Initial impact of the Fast Track prevention trial for conduct problems: I. The high-risk sample. *Journal of Consulting and Clinical Psychology*, **67**, 631–647.

Conduct Problems Prevention Research Group (2002). Using the fast track randomized prevention trial to test the early starter model of the development of serious conduct problems. *Development and Psychopathology*, **14**, 925–943.

Conger, R. D., Wallace, L. E., Sun, Y. M., Simons, R. L., McLoyd, V. C., & Brody, G. H. (2002). Economic pressure in African American families: A replication and extension of the family stress model. *Developmental Psychology*, **38**, 179–193.

Cote, S., Tremblay, R. E., Nagin, D., Zoccolillo, M., & Vitaro, F. (2002). The development of impulsivity, fearfulness, and helpfulness during childhood: Patterns of consistency and change in the trajectories of boys and girls. *Journal of Child Psychology and Psychiatry*, **43**, 609–618.

Cowan, P. A., & Cowan, C. P. (2002). Interventions as tests of family systems theories: Marital and family relationships in children's development and psychopathology. *Development and Psychopathology*, **14**, 731–759.

Crick, N. R. (1995). Relational aggression: The role of intent attributions, feelings of distress, and provocation type. *Development and Psychopathology*, **7**, 313–322.

Crick, N. R., Bigbee, M. A., & Howes, C. (1996). Gender differences in children's normative beliefs about aggression: How do I hurt thee? Let me count the ways. *Child Development*, **67**, 1003–1014.

Crick, N. R., Casas, J. F., & Nelson, D. A. (2002). Toward a more comprehensive understanding of peer maltreatment: Studies of relational victimization. *Current Directions in Psychological Science*, **11**, 98–101.

122

Criss, M. M., Pettit, G. S., Bates, J. E., Dodge, K. A., & Lapp, A. L. (2002). Family adversity, positive peer relationships, and children's externalizing behavior: A longitudinal perspective on risk and resilience. *Child Development*, **73**, 1220–1237.

Cummings, E. M., Davies, P. T., & Campbell, S. B. (2000). *Developmental psychopathology and family process*. New York: Guilford.

Dearing, E., McCartney, K., & Taylor, B. A. (2001). Change in family income-to-needs matters more for children with less. *Child Development*, **72**, 1779–1793.

Deater-Deckard, K., Dodge, K. A., Bates, J. E., & Pettit, G. S. (1998). Multiple risk factors in the development of externalizing behavior problems: Group and individual differences. *Development and Psychopathology*, **10**, 469–493.

Denham, S. A., Workman, E., Cole, P. M., Weissbrod, C., Kendziora, K. T., & Zahn-Waxler, C. (2000). Prediction of externalizing behavior problems from early to middle childhood: The role of parental socialization and emotional expression. *Development and Psychopathology*, **12**, 23–45.

Dishion, T. J., Andrews, D. W., & Crosby, L. (1995). Antisocial boys and their friends in early adolescence: Relationship characteristics, quality, and interaction process. *Child Development*, **66**, 139–151.

Duncan, G. J., Brooks-Gunn, J., & Klebanov, P. K. (1994). Economic deprivation and early childhood development. *Child Development*, **65**, 296–318.

Eisenberg, N., & Fabes, R. (1998). Prosocial development. In N. Eisenberg (Ed.) (Editor-in-Chief: W. Damon), *Social, emotional, and personality development. Vol. 3: Handbook of child psychology* (5th ed., pp. 701–778). New York: Wiley.

Fergusson, D. M., Lynskey, M. T., & Horwood, L. J. (1996). Factors associated with continuity and changes in disruptive behavior patterns between childhood and adolescence. *Journal of Abnormal Child Psychology*, **24**, 533–553.

Forehand, R., Armistead, L., & David, C. (1997). Is adolescent adjustment following parental divorce a function of predivorce adjustment? *Journal of Abnormal Child Psychology*, **25**, 157–164.

Garmezy, N. (1974). Children at risk: The search for the antecedents of schizophrenia: II. Ongoing research programs, issues, and intervention. *Schizophrenia Bulletin*, **9**, 55–125.

Garmezy, N. (1993). Children in poverty: Resilience despite risk. *Psychiatry: Interpersonal and Biological Processes*, **56**, 127–136.

Greenberg, M. T., Lengua, L. J., Coie, J. D., Pinderhughes, E. E., Bierman, K., Dodge, K. A., Lochman, J. E., & McMahon, R. J. (1999). Predicting developmental outcomes at school entry using a multiple-risk model: Four American communities. *Developmental Psychology*, **35**, 403–417.

Greenberg, M. T., Speltz, M. L., & DeKlyen, M. (1993). The role of attachment in the development of disruptive behavior problems. *Development and Psychopathology*, **5**, 191–214.

Greenberger, E., & Goldberg, W. A. (1989). Work, parenting, and the socialization of children. *Developmental Psychology*, **25**, 22–35.

Gresham, F. M., & Elliot, S. N. (1991). *Social skills rating system*. Circle Pines, MN: American Guidance Service.

Gutman, L. M., Sameroff, A. J., & Cole, R. (2003). Academic growth curve trajectories from 1st grade to 12th grade: Effects of multiple social risk factors and preschool child factors. *Developmental Psychology*, **39**, 777–790.

Halperin, J. M., Sharma, V., Greenblatt, E., & Schwartz, S. T. (1991). Assessment of the continuous performance test: Reliability and validity in a nonreferred sample. *Psychological Assessment: Journal of Consulting and Clinical Psychology*, **3**, 603–608.

Hart, D., Atkins, R., & Fegley, S. (2003). Personality and development in childhood: A person-centered approach. *Monographs of the Society for Research in Child Development*, **68** (Whole No. 272).

Hartup, W. W. (1974). Aggression in childhood: Developmental perspectives. *American Psychologist*, **29**, 337–341.

Hartup, W. W. (1996). The company they keep: Friendships and their developmental significance. *Child Development*, **67**, 1–13.

Hartup, W. W., Laursen, B., Stewart, M. A., & Eastenson, A. (1988). Conflicts and friendship relations of young children. *Child Development*, **59**, 1590–1600.

Hay, D. F., Castle, J., & Davies, L. (2000). Toddlers' use of force against familiar peers: A precursor of serious aggression? *Child Development*, **71**, 457–467.

Huesmann, L. R., Eron, L. D., Lefkowitz, M. M., & Walder, L. O. (1984). Stability of aggression over time and generations. *Developmental Psychology*, **20**, 1120–1134.

Jensen, P. S., Martin, D., & Cantwell, D. P. (1997). Comorbidity in ADHD: Implications for research, practice, and DSM-V. *Journal of the American Academy of Child and Adolescent Psychiatry*, **36**, 1065–1079.

Keenan, K., & Shaw, D. (1997). Developmental and social influences on young girls' early problem behavior. *Psychological Bulletin*, **121**, 95–113.

Kilgore, K., Snyder, J., & Lentz, C. (2000). The contribution of parental discipline, parental monitoring, and school risk to early-onset conduct problems in African American boys and girls. *Developmental Psychology*, **36**, 835–845.

Kochanska, G. (1995). Children's temperament, mother's discipline, and security of attachment: Multiple pathways to emerging internalization. *Child Development*, **66**, 597–615.

Kochanska, G. (1997). Multiple pathways to conscience for children with different temperaments: From toddlerhood to age 5. *Developmental Psychology*, **33**, 228–240.

Kochenderfer, B. J., & Ladd, G. W. (1996). Peer victimization: Cause or consequence of school maladjustment? *Child Development*, **67**, 1305–1317.

Koot, H. M. (1993). *Problem behavior in Dutch preschoolers*. Rotterdam: Erasmus University.

Koot, H. M., Van Den Oord, E. J., Verhulst, F. C., & Boomsma, D. I. (1997). Behavioral and emotional problems in young preschoolers: Cross-cultural testing of the validity of the child behavior checklist/2–3. *Journal of Abnormal Child Psychology*, **25**, 183–196.

Kopp, C. B. (1989). Regulation of distress and negative emotions: A developmental view. *Developmental Psychology*, **25**, 343–354.

Ladd, G. W., & Profilet, S. M. (1996). The child behavior scale: A teacher-report measure of young children's aggressive, withdrawn, and prosocial behaviors. *Developmental Psychology*, **32**, 1008–1024.

Lahey, B. B., Waldman, I. D., & McBurnett, K. (1999). The development of antisocial behavior: An integrative causal model. *Journal of Child Psychology and Psychiatry*, **40**, 669–682.

Lavigne, L. V., Arend, R., Rosenbaum, D., Binns, H. J., Christoffel, K. K., & Gibbons, R. D. (1998). Psychiatric disorder with onset in the preschool years: II. Correlates and predictors of stable case status. *Journal of the American Academy of Child and Adolescent Psychiatry*, **37**, 1255–1261.

Liang, K. Y., & Zeger, S. L. (1986). Longitudinal data analysis using generalized linear models. *Biometrika*, **73**, 13–22.

Liaw, F. R., & Brooks-Gunn, J. (1994). Cumulative familial risks and low-birth-weight children's cognitive and behavioral development. *Journal of Clinical Child Psychology*, **23**, 360–372.

Loeber, R., & Farrington, D. P. (2000). Young children who commit crime: Epidemiology, developmental origins, risk factors, early interventions, and policy implications. *Development and Psychopathology*, **12**, 737–762.

Loeber, R., Farrington, D. P., Stouthamer-Loeber, M., Moffitt, T. E., & Caspi, A. (1998). The development of male offending: Key findings from the first decade of the Pittsburgh youth study. *Studies on Crime and Prevention*, **7**, 141–171.

Loeber, R., Green, S. M., Lahey, B., & Kalb, L. (2000). Physical fighting in childhood as a risk factor for later mental health problems. *Journal of the American Academy Child and Adolescent Psychiatry*, **39**, 421–428.

Loeber, R., & Stouthamer-Loeber, M. (1998). Development of juvenile aggression and violence: Some common misperceptions and controversies. *American Psychologist*, **53**, 242–259.

Loeber, R., Tremblay, R. E., Gagnon, C., & Charlebois, P. (1989). Continuity and desistance in disruptive boys' early fighting at school. *Development and Psychopathology*, **1**, 39–50.

Love, J. M., Harrison, L., Sagi-Schwartz, A., van IJzendoorn, M. H., Ross, C., Ungerer, J. A., Raikes, H., Brady-Smith, C., Boller, K., Brooks-Gunn, J., Constantine, J., Kisker, E. E., Paulsell, D., & Chanzan-Cohen, R. (2003). Child care quality matters: How conclusions may vary with context. *Child Development*, **74**, 1021–1033.

Loeb, S., Fuller, B., Kagan, S. L., & Carrol, B. (2004). Child care in poor communities: Early learning effects of type, quality, and stability. *Child Development*, **75**, 47–65.

Luthar, S. S., Cicchetti, D., & Becker, B. (2000a). The construct of resilience: A critical evaluation and guidelines for future work. *Child Development*, **71**, 543–562.

Luthar, S. S., Cicchetti, D., & Becker, B. (2000b). Research on resilience: Response to commentaries. *Child Development*, **71**, 573–575.

Maccoby, E. E. (1998). *The two sexes: Growing up apart, coming together*. Cambridge, MA: Harvard University Press.

Maccoby, E. E., & Martin, J. A. (1983). Socialization in the context of the family: Parent-child interaction. In E. M. Hetherington (Ed.) (Editor-in-Chief: P. H. Mussen), *Socialization, personality, and social development. Vol. 4: Handbook of child psychology* (4th ed., pp. 1–101). New York: Wiley.

Masten, A. S., & Coatsworth, J. D. (1995). Competence, resilience and psychopathology. In D. Cicchetti & D. J. Cohen (Eds.), *Developmental psychopathology, vol. 2: Risk, disorder, and adaptation* (pp. 715–752). New York: Wiley.

Masten, A. S., & Coatsworth, J. D. (1998). The development of competence in favorable and unfavorable environments: Lessons from research on successful children. *American Psychologist*, **53**, 205–220.

Masten, A. S., Hubbard, J. J., Gest, S. D., Tellegen, A., Garmezy, N., & Ramirez, M. (1999). Competence in the context of adversity: Pathways to resilience and maladaptation from childhood to late adolescence. *Development and Psychopathology*, **11**, 143–169.

McLoyd, V. C. (1990). The impact of economic hardship on Black families and children: Psychological distress, parenting and socio-emotional development. *Child Development*, **61**, 311–346.

McLoyd, V. C. (1998). Socioeconomic disadvantage and child development. *American Psychologist*, **53**, 185–204.

Moffitt, T. E. (1990). Juvenile delinquency and attention deficit disorder: Boys' developmental trajectories from age 3 to age 15. *Child Development*, **61**, 893–910.

Moffitt, T. E. (1993). Adolescent-limited and life-course-persistent antisocial behavior: A developmental taxonomy. *Psychological Review*, **100**, 674–701.

Moffitt, T. E., Caspi, A., Dickson, N., Silva, P., & Stanton, W. (1996). Childhood-onset versus adolescent-onset antisocial conduct problems in males: Natural history from ages 3 to 18. *Development and Psychopathology*, **8**, 399–424.

Nagin, D. S. (1999). Analyzing developmental trajectories: A semiparametric, group-based approach. *Psychological Methods*, **4**, 139–157.

Nagin, D. S., & Tremblay, R. E. (1999). Trajectories of boys' physical aggression, opposition, and hyperactivity on the path to physically violent and nonviolent juvenile delinquency. *Child Development*, **70**, 1181–1196.

Nagin, D. S., & Tremblay, R. E. (2001). Parental and early childhood predictors of persistent physical aggression in boys from kindergarten to high school. *Archives of General Psychiatry*, **58**, 389–394.

NICHD Early Child Care Research Network (1997). The effects of infant child care on infant-mother attachment security: Results of the NICHD Study of Early Child Care. *Child Development*, **68**, 860–879.

NICHD Early Child Care Research Network (1998). Early child care and self-control: Compliance and problem behavior at twenty-four and thirty-six months. *Child Development*, **69**, 1145–1170.

NICHD Early Child Care Research Network (2000a). The relation of child care to cognitive and language development. *Child Development*, **71**, 960–980.

NICHD Early Child Care Research Network (2000b). Characteristics and quality of child care for toddlers and preschoolers. *Applied Developmental Science*, **4**, 116–135.

NICHD Early Child Care Research Network (2001a). Child care and children's peer interaction at 24 and 36 months: The NICHD Study of Early Child Care. *Child Development*, **72**, 1478–1500.

NICHD Early Child Care Research Network (2001b). Nonmaternal care and family factors in early development: An overview of the NICHD Study of Early Child Care. *Applied Developmental Psychology*, **22**, 457–492.

NICHD Early Child Care Research Network (2001c). A new guide for evaluating child care quality. *Bulletin of Zero to Three: National Center for Infants, Toddlers, and Families*, **21**, 40–47.

NICHD Early Child Care Research Network (2002). Early child care and children's development prior to school entry: Results from NICHD Study of Early Child Care. *American Educational Research Journal*, **39**, 133–164.

NICHD Early Child Care Research Network (2003a). Does the amount of time spent in child care predict socioemotional adjustment during the transition to kindergarten? *Child Development*, **74**, 976–1005.

NICHD Early Child Care Research Network (2003b). Does quality of child care affect child outcomes at age 4 1/2? *Developmental Psychology*, **39**, 451–469.

NICHD Early Child Care Research Network (2004). Affective dysregulation in the mother–child relationship in the toddler years: Antecedents and consequences. *Development and Psychopathology*, **16**, 43–68.

O'Connor, T. G., Deater-Deckard, K., Fulker, D., Rutter, M., & Plomin, R. (1998). Genotype-environment correlations in late childhood and early adolescence: Antisocial behavioral problems and coercive parenting. *Developmental Psychology*, **34**, 970–981.

Olweus, D. (1979). Stability of aggressive reaction patterns in males: A review. *Psychological Bulletin*, **86**, 852–875.

Parker, J. G., & Asher, S. R. (1987). Peer relations and later personal adjustment: Are low-accepted children at risk? *Psychological Bulletin*, **102**, 357–389.

Parker, J. G., & Asher, S. R. (1993). Friendship and friendship quality in middle childhood: Links with peer group acceptance and feelings of loneliness and dissatisfaction. *Developmental Psychology*, **29**, 611–621.

Patterson, G. R., DeBaryshe, B. D., & Ramsey, E. (1989). A developmental perspective on antisocial behavior. *American Psychologist*, **44**, 329–335.

Patterson, G. R., DeGarmo, D. S., & Knutson, N. (2000). Hyperactive and antisocial behaviors: Comorbid or two points in the same process? *Development and Psychopathology*, **12**, 91–106.

126

Patterson, G. R., Reid, J. B., & Dishion, T. J. (1992). *A social learning approach: IV. Antisocial boys*. Eugene, OR: Castalia.

Pelham, W. E. Jr., Gnagy, E. M., Greenslade, K. E., & Milich, R. (1992). Teacher ratings of DSM-III-R symptoms for the disruptive behavior disorders. *Journal of the American Academy of Child and Adolescent Psychiatry*, **32**, 210–219.

Pettit, G. S., Bates, J. E., & Dodge, K. A. (1997). Supportive parenting, ecological context, and children's adjustment: A seven-year longitudinal study. *Child Development*, **68**, 908–923.

Pettit, G. S., Laird, R. D., Dodge, K. A., Bates, J. E., & Criss, M. M. (2001). Antecedents and behavior-problem outcomes of parental monitoring and psychological control in early adolescence. *Child Development*, **72**, 583–598.

Pianta, R. C. (2001). *Student-Teacher Relationship Scale*. Odessa, FL: PAR.

Pierce, E. W., Ewing, L. J., & Campbell, S. B. (1999). Diagnostic status and symptomatic behavior of hard-to-manage preschool children in middle childhood and early adolescence. *Journal of Clinical Child Psychology*, **28**, 44–57.

Radloff, L. (1977). The CES-D Scale: A self-report depression scale for research in the general population. *Journal of Applied Psychological Measurement*, **1**, 385–401.

Reynell, J. (1991). *Reynell Developmental Language Scales (U. S. edition)*. Los Angeles: Western Psychological Service.

Richman, N., Stevenson, J., & Graham, P. J. (1982). *Pre-school to school: A behavioral study*. London: Academic Press.

Rosvold, H. E., Mirsky, A. G., Sarason, I., Bransome, E. D. Jr., & Beck, L. H. (1956). A continuous performance test of brain damage. *Journal of Consulting Psychology*, **20**, 343–350.

Rubin, K. H., Bukowski, W., & Parker, J. G. (1998). Peer interactions, relationships, and groups. In N. Eisenberg (Ed.) (Editor-in-Chief: W. Damon), *Social, emotional, and personality development. Vol. 3: Handbook of child psychology* (5th ed., pp. 619–700). New York: Wiley.

Rubin, K. H., Burgess, K. B., Dwyer, K. M., & Hastings, P. D. (2003). Predicting preschoolers' externalizing behaviors from toddler temperament, conflict, and maternal negativity. *Developmental Psychology*, **39**, 164–176.

Rutter, M. (1979). Protective factors in children's responses to stress and disadvantage. In M. W. Kent & J. E. Rolf (Eds.), *Primary prevention of psychopathology: Vol. 3. Social competence in children* (pp. 49–74). Hanover, NH: University Press of New England.

Rutter, M. (1987). Psychosocial resilience and protective mechanisms. *American Journal of Orthopsychiatry*, **57**, 316–331.

Sameroff, A. J. (2000). Dialectical processes in developmental psychopathology. In A. J. Sameroff, M. Lewis & S. Miller (Eds.), *Handbook of developmental psychopathology* (2nd ed., pp. 23–40). New York: Plenum Press.

Sameroff, A. J., Bartko, W. T., Baldwin, A., Baldwin, C., & Seifer, R. (1998). Family and social influences on the development of child competence. In M. Lewis & C. Fiering (Eds.), *Families, risk and competence* (pp. 161–185). Mahwah, NJ: Lawrence Erlbaum Associates.

Sameroff, A. J., Seifer, R., Baldwin, A., & Baldwin, C. P. (1993). Stability of intelligence from preschool to adolescence: The influence of social and family risk factors. *Child Development*, **64**, 80–97.

Shaefer, E. S., & Edgerton, M. (1985). Parent and child correlates of parental modernity. In I. E. Sigel (Ed.), *Parental belief systems* (pp. 287–318). Hillsdale, NJ: Erlbaum.

Shantz, C. U. (1987). Conflicts between children. *Child Development*, **58**, 282–305.

Shaw, D. S., Bell, R. Q., & Gilliom, M. (2000). A truly early starter model of antisocial behavior revisited. *Clinical Child and Family Psychology Review*, **3**, 155–172.

Shaw, D. S., Gilliom, M., Ingoldsby, E. M., & Nagin, D. S. (2003). Trajectories leading to school-age conduct problems. *Developmental Psychology*, **39**, 189–200.

Shaw, D. S., Owens, E. B., Vondra, J. I., Keenan, K., & Winslow, E. B. (1996). Early risk factors and pathways in the development of early disruptive behavior problems. *Development and Psychopathology*, **8**, 679–699.

Shaw, D. S., Vondra, J. I., Dowdell-Hommerding, K. D., Keenan, K., & Dunn, M. (1994). Chronic family adversity and early child-behavior problems: A longitudinal study of low-income families. *Journal of Child Psychology and Psychiatry*, **35**, 1109–1122.

Shaw, D. S., Winslow, E. B., Owens, E. B., Vondra, J. I., Cohn, J. F., & Bell, R. Q. (1998). The development of early externalizing problems among children from low-income families: A transformational perspective. *Journal of Abnormal Child Psychology*, **26**, 95–107.

Singer, J. D., & Willett, J. B. (2003). *Applied longitudinal data analysis: Modeling change and event occurrence*. London: Oxford University Press.

Spieker, S. J., Larson, N. C., Lewis, S. M., Keller, T. E., & Gilchrist, L. (1999). Developmental trajectories of disruptive behavior problems in preschool children of adolescent mothers. *Child Development*, **70**, 443–458.

Stouthamer-Loeber, M., Loeber, R., Farrington, D. P., Zhang, Q. W., Van Kammen, W., & Maguin, E. (1993). The double edge of protective and risk-factors for delinquency: Interrelations and developmental patterns. *Development and Psychopathology*, **5**, 683–701.

Strassberg, Z., Dodge, K. A., Pettit, G. S., & Bates, J. E. (1994). Spanking in the home and children's subsequent aggression toward kindergarten peers. *Development and Psychopathology*, **6**, 445–462.

Thompson, R. A. (1998). Early socio-personality development. In N. Eisenberg (Ed.) (Editor-in-Chief: W. Damon), *Social, emotional and personality development. Vol. 3: Handbook of child psychology* (5th ed., pp. 25–140). New York: Wiley.

Tremblay, R. E. (2000). The development of aggressive behavior during childhood: What have we learned in the past century? *International Journal of Behavioral Development*, **24**, 129–141.

Tremblay, R. E., Pihl, R. O., Vitaro, F., & Dobkin, P. L. (1994). Predicting early-onset of male antisocial-behavior from preschool behavior. *Archives of General Psychiatry*, **51**, 732–739.

Vitaro, F., Brendgen, M., & Tremblay, R. E. (1999). Prevention of school dropout through the reduction of disruptive behaviors and school failure in elementary school. *Journal of School Psychology*, **37**, 205–226.

Votruba-Drzal, E., Coley, R. L., & Chase-Lansdale, P. L. (2004). Child care and low-income children's development: Direct and moderated effects. *Child Development*, **75**, 296–312.

Werner, E., & Smith, S. (1977). *Kauai's children come of age*. Honolulu: University of Hawaii Press.

Winer, B. J. (1971). *Statistical principles in experimental design* (2nd ed.). New York: McGraw-Hill.

Woodcock, R. W., & Johnson, M. B. (1989). *Woodcock-Johnson Psycho-Educational Battery-Revised*. Allen, TX: DLM Teaching Resources.

Woodcock, R. W., & Johnson, M. B. (1990). *Woodcock-Johnson Psycho-Educational Battery-Revised*. Allen, TX: DLM Teaching Resources.

Zimmerman, I. L., Steiner, V. G., & Pond, R. E. (1992). *Preschool Language Scale-3*. San Antonio, TX: The Psychological Corporation.

ACKNOWLEDGMENTS

We express our appreciation to our study coordinators and research assistants who oversaw and collected the data, and to the children, families, teachers, and child-care providers who have participated so willingly in this longitudinal study.

Correspondence concerning this article should be addressed to NICHD Early Child Care Research Network, CRMC, NICHD, 6100 Executive Boulevard, 4B05, Rockville, MD 20852, USA.

COMMENTARY

THE STABILITY OF YOUNG CHILDREN'S PHYSICAL AGGRESSION: RELATIONS WITH CHILD CARE, GENDER, AND AGGRESSION SUBTYPES

William F. Arsenio

This *Monograph* by the Early Child Care Research Network (ECCRN) is another in a series of major contributions to emerge from this unique collaborative effort. Originally, this project was funded by the National Institute of Child Health and Human Development (NICHD) to address the need for a comprehensive study that could answer many of the unresolved questions regarding the short- and long-term effects of early nonmaternal child care on children's developmental trajectories. Although many of the dozens of subsequent ECCRN publications have had a primary focus on the effects of nonmaternal care, the wealth of data from this continuing project has led to important investigations of a number of related topics, including the present investigation of the trajectories of physical aggression in young children.

The authors of this *Monograph* used longitudinal data from the ECCRN project to assess patterns of physical aggression up to the age of 8 years, and, in their words, the predictors, causes, and correlates of that aggression. A composite measure of children's maternally rated physical aggression was formed based on six items from the Child Behavior Checklist (CBCL, Achenbach, 1991, 1992) involving children's overt harm to others and physical destruction of objects. Person-centered analyses conducted using multiple CBCL assessments from when children were 24 months old through third grade revealed five separable groups with distinct development trajectories. In four groups, including high, moderate, and two low-aggression groups, children's relative level of physical aggression stayed quite stable over a 6-year period. In addition, a fifth group was identified that was moderately aggressive at 24 months, but then steeply declined in aggression between 36 and 54 months and remained low.

The analyses and discussion regarding the antecedents and correlates of these different aggression trajectories provide a remarkable, fine-grained picture of how patterns of childhood aggression emerge. In this commentary, I want to highlight just a few of these major contributions, with a particular focus on issues of stability of aggression and the importance of identifying the unique group, which exhibited moderate and then declining aggression. Following this, I want to bring the discussion back to the initial focus of the ECCRN project, that is, the connections between nonmaternal child care and children's socioemotional development and adjustment. Two final topics involve unanswered questions about gender and aggression, and the emergence of different subtypes of aggression.

TRAJECTORIES OF PHYSICAL AGGRESSION

One of the major contributions of this *Monograph* is what it reveals about the emergence of stable trajectories in 2- through 8-year-old children's patterns of aggression. There has been some debate in the aggression literature regarding Olweus's (1979) provocative early review in which he summarized studies suggesting that long-term patterns of childhood aggression were as stable as patterns of intelligence. By contrast, Loeber and Stouthamer-Loeber (1998) argue that narrow interpretations of this stability claim have led to a major misconception in the study of children's aggression and violence, namely that high levels of stability in aggression over time necessarily mean that there is a "negligible" amount of discontinuity of aggression from adulthood to early childhood. They argue that researchers also need to focus on desistance and escalation, as well as persistence, in children's aggression trajectories (see also Loeber, Tremblay, Gagnon, & Charlebois, 1989).

The authors of this *Monograph* were, of course, well aware of the importance of this issue when they made it a central focus of their project. Much of their literature review summarizes previous studies that tracked the developmental trajectories of aggressive children, as well as key questions left unanswered by that work. For example, one especially notable project (Broidy et al., 2003) included results from a six-site cross-national comparison that followed developmental trajectories in children's physical aggression beginning at age 6 or 7 through early adolescence. Several groups could be identified, including, for boys, a major group that was initially low in physical aggression and that declined even more by 11–13 years (almost 90–95% in all samples) and another small, highly aggressive group (from 4% to 11% across samples) that remained high in physical aggression during adolescence (and increased in samples from the United States). Although an even greater majority of girls revealed little or no physical aggression, it was still possible to identify a stable group of highly aggressive girls. Finally, there was no evidence for a group that started low in physical aggression and then increased to even moderate levels of aggression in adolescence.

These results reveal that similar, relatively stable patterns of physical aggression appear to emerge in children from a number of countries (Canada, New Zealand, and the United States) beginning in elementary school and continuing through early adolescence. Yet, as Tremblay (2000) observed, these findings (e.g., Nagin & Tremblay, 1999) immediately raise another question. Given that aggression was first examined in these studies when children were 6, and aggression patterns were already stable by that age, exactly when did stable developmental trajectories of these aggressive patterns *first* emerge? This is precisely the question that the present *Monograph* sought to answer.

Based on the person-centered analyses, the *Monograph* authors identified five distinct trajectories in young children's physical aggression from age 2 through 8, including two stable, but low trajectories (including 70% of the sample) and two stable, high trajectories (18% of the sample). In other words, for nearly 90% of the sample, early trajectories in physical aggression were surprisingly stable, beginning at perhaps the earliest age that differences in physical aggression can be measured. At the same time, however, about 12% of children who initially had moderate levels of physical aggression at 24 months (between the two high and the two low aggression groups) showed a steep decline in aggression between 36 and 54 months. Between the age of 2 and 8 years, then, there is both a high level of stability in most children's physical aggression, as well as a major decline in physical aggression for some children. Although these findings are limited to young children, they provide initial support for both Olweus's (1979) claim regarding the developmental stability of aggression as well as Loeber and Stouthamer–Loeber's argument for nontrivial discontinuities in at least some aggression trajectories.

The identification of the moderate, then steeply declining aggression group is arguably one of the most intriguing findings in this *Monograph*. Although one other study found patterns of aggression desistance in this age group (Shaw, Gilliom, Nagin, & Ingoldsby, 2003), the emergence of a steeply declining aggression group in a mixed gender, socioeconomically representative group is unique. All of this leads to the question, what makes this group unique? What family, sociodemographic, or other factors could lead to such a decline? And, at an intervention level, can anything be learned from this group that could prove useful for altering the aggression trajectories of the stable moderate and high aggression groups?

Unfortunately, none of these questions can be answered. Even though the *Monograph* included a broad range of risk and promotive factors, and analyses assessing both composite measures of risk as well as potentially separable contributors, there was little to distinguish the steeply declining group from the moderate stable or other aggression trajectory groups. This inability to characterize the special qualities associated with the steeply declining group is especially surprising given that the demographic and family measures were otherwise very effective at predicting children's aggression group membership. Increased levels of family risk (including lower income and maternal education), in general, had linear relations with children's aggression group status. Moreover, lower levels of observed maternal sensitivity and maternal reports of more depressive symptoms and less child-centered attitudes were associated with children's membership in higher aggression groups. Finally, family risk factors measured *after* children were 24 months old (i.e., up to age 8) added very little to the prediction of childhood aggression, a finding that stemmed from the high level of stability in family risk factors over the 8 years of this study. In other words, changes in risk factors could not predict changes in aggression because there was very little change in those risk factors.

None of these findings explain why 12% of the children started out moderately high in aggression and then declined rapidly in preschool years, but they do help to explain the stability of the aggression trajectories of the other 88% of the children. And other studies underscore that there is nothing particularly unusual about this 8-year level of stability. Take, for example, the Rochester study (Sameroff, 1996; Sameroff, Seifer, Baldwin, & Baldwin, 1993) which followed changes in the children's cognitive and socioemotional functioning over a 14-year period in relation to a set of now commonly studied risk and protective factors (e.g., maternal education, parental sensitivity, etc). When children were 4 years old, these risk factors accounted for nearly half of the variability in their cognitive functioning and a quarter of their socioemotional functioning. Longitudinal assessments when children were 13 and 18 years old also revealed a strong linear relation between the cumulative number of risk factors and adolescents' outcomes. Unexpectedly to these authors, however, there very few major changes in the number of risk factors and children's risk profiles across a 14-year period (from when children were 4–18 years old). Based on other analyses from this project and related studies, Sameroff concluded that it was not the presence of any single risk factor, but rather the combination of tightly clustered risk factors that are especially damaging to children's development. "Perhaps we can maximize the efficiency of intervention efforts when we realize that it is not being poor alone, or living in a bad neighborhood alone, or having a single parent alone that places children at risk, but rather the *combination* of these factors that sap the lives of families" (Sameroff, 1996, p. 8 [emphasis in the original]).

One implication of this understandable emphasis on multiple, converging risk factors is that interventions that target a single factor, whether maternal education or poverty, are seen as unlikely to have a major effect on

133

children's long-term developmental trajectories. Yet results from a recent large-scale naturalistic experiment (Costello, Compton, Keeler, & Angold, 2003) provide a somewhat different view. The 8-year longitudinal Great Smoky Mountains Study was designed to track the development of psychiatric disorders and access to mental health facilities in a sample of more than 1,400 children (aged 9, 11, and 13 at intake) and their parents and caregivers in western North Carolina. About $\frac{1}{4}$ of the child participants were Native American, with most of the rest from European American backgrounds. Once a year, from the beginning of the study in 1993 through 2000, child participants and their parents or guardians were given structured assessments (the Child and Adolescent Psychiatric Assessment) that were used to derive broad measures of emotional disorders (depression and anxiety) and behavioral disorders (oppositional defiant disorder and conduct disorder). Adult respondents also provided information about family income.

About 3 years into the study, a gambling casino was built on the tribal reservation, resulting in a major increase in the number of jobs available as well as direct profit sharing payments to all Native Americans, payments that increased up to $6,000 a year (for every adult and child) over a several-year period. Using federal poverty guidelines, the percentage of poor Native American families dropped from more than 50% in 1993 to under 25% in 2000, whereas non-Native American families experienced a much smaller decline in poverty rates (from about 25% to 20%).

Study findings revealed that, overall (across all 8 years of the study), there were significant connections between family income and children's psychiatric symptoms for both Native and non-Native American groups. Perhaps more importantly, increases in the income for Native Americans during this time were also associated with declines in children's psychiatric symptoms, but this was mostly true for one particular subgroup. Using federal poverty guidelines, some families were designated as persistently poor (i.e., poor before and after the casino was built), some as ex-poor (poor before but not after the casino), and some as never poor (either before or after the casino). The largest change occurred in the ex-poor group where children and adolescents showed a 40% decline in total psychiatric symptoms and behavior problems. In fact, children in the ex-poor group saw their total problem scores drop to the same level as children from never poor families.

Subsequent analyses addressed the potential mechanisms underlying these dramatic changes. It was found that improvements in parents' monitoring and supervision of their children's activities were responsible for mediating the connections between increasing family income and declining child and adolescent psychiatric symptoms (accounting for 77% of the observed effect). Finally, exploratory analyses pointed to three specific changes related to improvements in ex-poor parents' supervision of their children: a decline in the number of single parent families; an increase in households with working parents; and a decline in time demands on parents (see Jacobson & Crockett, 2000; and, Lamborn, Mounts, Steinberg, & Dornbusch, 1991, on the effects of parental monitoring on adolescents' psychosocial functioning).

What is especially striking about these findings is that they suggest that changing a single risk factor such as family income can, in fact, have a major effect on the trajectory of children's development, including specific changes in "behavior problems" (e.g., conduct disorders) that are relevant for the patterns of physical aggression assessed in this *Monograph*. Although risk factors often covary in a relatively tight cluster, it may be that changes in poverty, and significant increases income, in particular, can set off a cascade of other changes. What is unclear from this project is whether it was increased income, per se, and/or the sudden increase in job opportunities that initiated the important changes in parental monitoring behaviors and resulting reduction of children's and adolescents' psychiatric symptoms.

In terms of this *Monograph*, there was no evidence for similar dramatic changes in income or other sociodemographic or family variables that could explain the rapid decline in aggression for the steeply declining group. The results of the Great Smoky Mountains study, however, do raise the possibility that substantial, although relatively circumscribed, changes in families risk profiles can have a major effect on children's externalizing problems. Hopefully, subsequent publications from the ECCRN project will target the steeply declining aggression group for even more intensive study, and the underlying causes for the early aggression desistance pattern can be identified.

DAY CARE AND AGGRESSION

Another important, if less obvious, contribution of this *Monograph* involves the findings linking nonmaternal child care and children's aggressive tendencies. As noted above, the NICHD Study of Early Child Care was initiated in the early 1990s to address the mixed findings that were emerging on the effects of nonmaternal child care on children's subsequent social–emotional and cognitive development. One underlying and continuing source of concern involves the rapid historical changes in women's workforce participation. For example, the percentage of women with children under the age of one in the workforce increased from 27% in 1970 (Kamerman, 2000) to 58% in 1998–1999 (Bureau of Labor Statistics, 2000). Given these enormous changes (and implicit cultural expectations about who is responsible for parenting and "domestic labor" [Silverstein, 1991]), questions were raised about how the timing (e.g., infant vs. later child care),

135

cumulative amount, and quality of nonmaternal child care all affect children.

Although the NICHD project has produced a number of publications on the effects on nonmaternal child care, one of the most prominent is a recent lead article in *Child Development* (NICHD Early Child Care Research Network, 2003), which was the subject of eight accompanying commentaries as well as an extensive editorial overview. The reasons for this level of attention are quite clear from the article's abstract. "The more time children spent in any variety of nonmaternal care arrangements across the first 4.5 years of life, the more externalizing problems and conflicts they manifested at 54 months and in kindergarten, as reported by mothers, caregivers, and teachers. These effects remained, for the most part, even when quality, type, and instability of child care were controlled, and when maternal sensitivity and other family background factors were taken into account" (p. 976). The authors acknowledged that the magnitude of these negative effects was relatively small, less than observed effects for maternal sensitivity or socioeconomic status. They concluded on a clear cautionary note, however, by discussing how even small effect sizes can have significant public policy implications, citing the utility of taking aspirin for preventing heart attacks (with an estimated r^2 of .001) as an example.

It was hard to ignore this evidence of the potentially damaging effects of any form of nonmaternal care, regardless of the amount or quality of care, especially coming from a study designed to be the "gold standard" in this area. Not surprisingly, the media were quick to pay attention, and there was another round in the long-standing national debate about nonmaternal child-care, women in the work force, and the nature and significance of changes in the structure of the family.

In light of this recent controversy, it is especially noteworthy that the longitudinal findings from the *Monograph* (which followed these children into third grade) are not consistent with the 2003 findings in several major ways. Using the same variable-centered approach used in the earlier report, this *Monograph* found that "fewer hours in care from infancy to 24 months predicted both higher levels of physical aggression at 24 months, and a slower decline in aggression. The children in the most child care initially were also lowest in physical aggression as noted by their mothers" (p. 123). Results from the person-centered analyses also provide a markedly different picture of the effects of nonmaternal care than the 2003 report. There were no significant connections between infants' (0–24 months) hours or quality of care and children's subsequent aggression trajectories once key covariates (e.g., family income) were controlled. Moreover, there were no linear connections between children's cumulative nonmaternal child between 24 and 54 months of age and their subsequent aggressive behavior. Children in the most aggressive groups neither received the most nonmaternal care, nor the greatest increases over time in nonmaternal care compared with other trajectory groups. In summary, "neither quality of care nor time in center was associated systematically with aggression trajectory in the person-centered analysis or with aggression level or rate of change in aggression in the variable centered-analysis. These results also differ from our earlier report" (p. 124).

What could explain these strikingly different findings from two articles based on the same longitudinal project? The *Monograph* authors briefly list several possibilities, including two candidates that are likely to be the focus of subsequent publications based on these data. One explanation involves differences in the raters used to assess physical aggression in these two reports, mothers only in this study vs. mothers, caregivers, and teachers once children began kindergarten in the 2003 study. As the *Monograph* authors note, teachers' and mothers' agreement on children's level of early aggression is often not high, both because of the potential situational specificity of aggression in young children, and because mothers and caregivers/teachers have different comparative frames of reference. This last suggestion could imply that teachers/caregivers, who are typically exposed to more children than mothers, are actually more *expert* at assessing relative levels of aggression—thus raising questions about maternal ratings.

The longitudinal findings from the *Monograph*, however, indicate that maternal ratings of children's physical aggression predicted an impressive array of children's social and cognitive outcomes in third grade. The maternal ratings-based aggression trajectories revealed that the two high-aggression groups were seen as less engaged and more disruptive by teachers, less engaged by independent classroom observers, more likely to describe themselves as lonely, and less competent across a great majority of relevant measures than the two low aggression groups. These third-grade outcome differences were both broad and deep, with the most aggressive groups described as "worse, often much worse across a range competence and behavior problem measures" (p. 94) than their less aggressive peers. Clearly, the predictive power of mothers' ratings of their children's aggressive tendencies was quite strong.

The most obvious alternative explanation for differences in the findings obtained from the 2003 report and this *Monograph* involves the different longitudinal intervals covered by these studies, that is, 0–5+ years in the 2003 report vs. 0–8 years in this report. One way of integrating these two distinct study intervals and their associated findings begins with the idea that the amount of nonmaternal child care that children experience prior to entering late preschool/kindergarten may be related to an initial "school adjustment bump" only. In other words, children exposed to more non-maternal child-care may initially seem problematic to their kindergarten teachers, but as these children move through school their socioemotional adjustment becomes indistinguishable from their peers with little or no history of nonmaternal care. In fact, such a pattern has been found in at least two studies (Egeland & Heister, 1995; Harvey, 1999).

Versions of this "adjustment bump" argument have had a long history in writings on the effects of day care. In her influential review of the effects of infant child care, for example, Clarke-Stewart (1989) acknowledged that some studies showed a connection between increased levels of early non-maternal care and greater childhood defiance and aggression. She also questioned, however, whether these findings might be an indirect effect of the *positive* effects of child-care experience such as greater independence, self-confidence, and a tendency to question the legitimacy of adult com-mands. Fortunately, the authors of the 2003 report were aware of these concerns: in addition to the physical aggression scale, they used other items from the CBCL to create measures of children's disobedience (e.g. "talks back to staff") as well as of their assertiveness (e.g., "talks too much", "de-mands attention"). Interestingly, it was found that although the total amount of nonmaternal child care was related to higher levels of caregiver/ teachers ratings on all three scales (when children were 54 months old and in kindergarten), children's time in child care was related to maternal rat-ings of *assertiveness* only (and just for kindergarten ratings). The findings from this *Monograph* suggest that mothers may not have been entirely wrong in their differentiated judgments of their children's behavior.

Many of the questions I have raised here are likely to be addressed as part of either "in press" or upcoming publications based on the NICHD data. But as the already extensive body of published studies grows, many developmental psychologists, policy analysts, and parents are likely to feel like the proverbial blind person trying to envision the whole elephant from necessarily incomplete explorations of the trunk, then the leg, etc. The authors of the *Monograph* and 2003 *Child Development* report are aware of this as both a general issue, and as it relates specifically to the effects of nonmaternal child care on children. To date, publications from the NICHD project have found that the significant connections between time spent in child care and children's socioemotional adjustment at 24 months disap-peared at 36 months (NICHD ECCRN, 1998), only to reappear by kin-dergarten (NICHD ECCRN, 2003), and then, as seen in this *Monograph*, to disappear again by third grade.

There is no other way the results of this massive, continuing project could be reported. Yet, given the original focus of this study on the lon-gitudinal effects of nonmaternal child care, and the charged cultural atmosphere in which those results will always emerge, it is essential that each new wave of longitudinal findings—whether mostly "positive" or "negative"—receives a similar level of attention within the field. None of this is meant as a criticism of the *Monograph*: its contributions to our understanding of the earliest emergence of stable patterns of physical aggression are unique and likely to have a major effect on the literature. Instead, it is meant as a reminder of the continuing need to attend to the public policy implications of this massive longitudinal project.

BEYOND PHYSICAL AGGRESSION

The focus on children's physical aggression in the *Monograph* is a clear methodological strength. As Tremblay (2000) and others have argued, the typical tendency to aggregate various types of aggressive, disruptive, and problematic behaviors into composite measures has sometimes made it difficult to predict meaningful developmental patterns of aggression. At the same time, moving from assessing broad "externalizing tendencies" to examining more discrete categories of aggression makes it possible to ignore other "aggression-related" behaviors that are developmentally problematic but not part of the target form of aggression being studied. I would like to conclude by addressing another distinct form of aggression that is more characteristic of girls, relational aggression, and with a brief discussion of the need to focus on the developmental origins of the reactive/proactive aggression distinction.

Relational Aggression

Extensive research programs by Crick and Underwood and their colleagues have focused on the distinction between overt, often physical, forms of aggression and more relational forms of aggression, that is, "harming others through purposeful manipulation and damage of their peer relationships" (Crick & Grotpeter, 1995, p. 771). Although a small number of girls are overtly aggressive, indirect and relational forms of aggression are both developmentally more normative for girls, and relational aggression is far more common for girls, accounting for up to 80% of those girls seen as aggressive by peers and teachers (Underwood, Galen, & Paquette, 2001). Moreover, girls who are identified as being more relationally aggressive by peers are subsequently more likely to be rated by teachers as showing a broad range of both externalizing and internalizing tendencies (e.g., Crick, 1997). Consequently, it is not surprising that only about $\frac{1}{4}$ of the children in the most aggressive group in the present study were girls, and that proportion of girls in each aggression group declined systematically, moving from the least to the most aggressive trajectory groups.

It is important to assess physical aggression in girls, especially given the evidence that a small, persistently aggressive group of girls is likely to experience outcomes similar to those of aggressive boys (e.g., Broidy et al.,

139

2003). An exclusive focus on physical aggression, however, will necessarily underestimate the severity and long-term consequences of the most common form of aggression found in girls. It would be useful if future analyses based on ECCRN data attempted to address this issue, perhaps by coding relational aggression from the available peer–peer observations (see, e.g., McNeilly-Choque, Hart, Robinson, Nelson, & Olsen, 1996), or by using some of the admittedly limited relevant information from the CBCL (e.g., items involving teasing and jealousy).

Reactive and Proactive Aggression

A final issue is what the present focus on physical aggression can reveal about the developmental origins of two major types of aggression, that is, reactive and proactive aggression. In general, reactive or "hot-headed" aggression has been associated with children's tendencies to misperceive others' intentions (i.e., a hostile attributional bias), whereas proactive or more "cold-blooded" aggression has been associated with a more deliberate use of aggression to achieve instrumental ends (see, e.g., Coie & Dodge, 1998, for a review). Despite a fair amount of overlap in these two forms of aggression, there is evidence that proactively aggressive children are more socially preferred by their peers than other types of aggressive children (Dodge, Lochman, Harnish, Bates, & Pettit, 1997) and that reactive, but not proactive, aggression is associated with lower verbal/cognitive abilities in adolescents (Arsenio, Gold, & Adams, in press).

Findings such as these have led to a debate about the different origins, functions, and consequences of reactive and proactive aggression. For example, Sutton, Smith, and Swettenham (1999) have argued that not all aggressive children are short-tempered "social oafs" and that some aggressive children are actually quite socially competent and skilled. By contrast, we (Arsenio & Lemerise, 2001) have argued that the lack of emotional responsiveness exhibited by proactively aggressive children toward their victims is likely to have substantial negative developmental consequences–consequences that may closely resemble those exhibited by children high in what Frick, Cornell, Bodin, Dane, Barry, and Loney (2003) have called callous–unemotional traits.

There has been very little research, to date, on the early developmental and familial origins of this important distinction between reactive and proactive aggression. Given that both forms of aggression are primarily physical in young children, however, analyses based on the present data could provide a unique understanding of how and when these types of aggression begin to diverge in children. Existing videotaped observational assessments could be coded both for emotional variables likely to be associated with reactive aggression (e.g., anger) and proactive aggression (e.g., inappropriate happiness), as well as the frequency with which these forms of aggression are displayed. Subsequent analyses could then address differential sociodemographic, familial, and other child-related variables that are more predictive of reactive and proactive aggression.

CONCLUSION

This impressive *Monograph* extends our understanding of the early origins of children's aggression in multiple ways. Using maternal ratings from the CBCL, it was possible to identify the emergence of different child aggression trajectories beginning at 24 months, an age when individual differences in physical aggression are just beginning to develop. Overall, the resulting trajectory groups revealed a surprising amount of stability in physical aggression across a 6-year period for most children, with the exception of the moderate then steeply declining aggression group. In addition, the *Monograph* findings revealed both how strongly sociodemographic, familial, and other related variables predicted these early trajectories, and how these aggressive trajectories, in turn, were predictive of a broad range of child-related outcomes at age 8. Other contributions are both methodological and substantive, including the ability to compare and contrast the different findings resulting from person- vs. variable-centered analyses. Finally, the authors have both clarified the literature on the early childhood aggression in major and lasting ways, and have also raised significant new questions for subsequent publications from the ECCRN project regarding child care and aggression and the underlying causes for the steeply declining aggression group.

References

Achenbach, T. (1991). *Manual for the child behavior checklist/4–18 and 1991 profile*. Burlington, VT: University of Vermont, Department of Psychiatry.
Achenbach, T. (1992). *Manual for the child behavior checklist/2–3 and 1992 profile*. Burlington, VT: University of Vermont, Department of Psychiatry.
Arsenio, W., Gold, J., & Adams, E. (in press). Adolescents' emotion expectancies regarding aggressive and nonaggressive events: Connections with behavior problems. *Journal of Experimental Child Psychology*.
Arsenio, W., & Lemerise, E. (2001). Varieties of childhood bullying: Values, emotion processes, and social competence. *Social Development*, **10**, 59–73.
Broidy, L., Nagin, D., Tremblay, R., Bates, J., Brame, B., Dodge, K., Fergusson, D., Horwood, J., Loeber, R., Laird, R., Lynam, D., Moffit, T., Pettit, G., & Vitaro, F. (2003). Developmental trajectories of childhood disruptive behaviors and adolescent delinquency: A six-site, cross-national study. *Developmental Psychology*, **39**, 222–245.
Bureau of Labor Statistics, U.S. Department of Labor. (2000). Does the amount of time spent in child care predict socioemotional adjustment during the transition to kindergarten. *Child Development*, **74**, 976–1005. Washington, DC: Author.

Clarke-Stewart, A. (1989). Infant daycare: Maligned or malignant? *American Psychologist*, **44**, 263–277.

Coie, J., & Dodge, K. (1998). Aggression and antisocial behavior. In W. Damon (Series Ed.) N. Eisenberg (Vol. Ed.), *Handbook of child psychology, Volume 3: Social, emotional, and personality development* (pp. 779–862). NY: Wiley.

Costello, E., Compton, S., Keeler, G., & Angold, A. (2003). Relationships between poverty and psychopathology: A natural experiment. *JAMA*, **290** (15), 2023–2029.

Crick, N. (1997). Engagement in gender normative versus gender nonnormative forms of adjustment: Links to social–psychological adjustment. *Developmental Psychology*, **33**, 610–617.

Crick, N., & Grotpeter, J. (1995). Relational aggression, gender, and social–psychological adjustment. *Child Development*, **66**, 710–722.

Dodge, K., Lochman, J., Harnish, J., Bates, J., & Pettit, G. (1997). Reactive and proactive aggression in school children and psychiatrically impaired chronically assaultive youth. *Journal of Abnormal Psychology*, **106**, 37–51.

Egeland, B., & Heister, M. (1995). The long-term consequences of infant day-care and mother–infant attachment. *Child Development*, **66**, 474–485.

Frick, P., Cornell, A., Bodin, D., Dane, H., Barry, C., & Loney, B. (2003). Callous–unemotional traits and developmental pathways to severe conduct problems. *Developmental Psychology*, **39**, 246–260.

Harvey, E. (1999). Short-term and long-term effects of parental employment on children of the National Longitudinal Survey of Youth. *Developmental Psychology*, **35**, 445–459.

Jacobson, K., & Crockett, L. (2000). Parental monitoring and adolescent adjustment: An ecological perspective. *Journal of Research on Adolescence*, **10**, 65–97.

Kamerman, S. (2000). Parental leave policies: An essential ingredient in early childhood education and care policies. *Social Policy Report*, **14**, 3–15.

Lamborn, S., Mounts, N., Steinberg, L., & Dornbusch, S. (1991). Patterns of competence and adjustment among adolescents from authoritative, authoritarian, indulgent, and neglectful families. *Child Development*, **62**, 1049–1065.

Loeber, R., & Stouthamer-Loeber, M. (1998). Development of juvenile aggression and violence: Some common misconceptions and controversies. *American Psychologist*, **53** (2), 242–259.

Loeber, R., Tremblay, R., Gagnon, C., & Charlebois, P. (1989). Continuity and desistance in disruptive boys' early fighting at school. *Development and Psychopathology*, **1**, 39–50.

McNeilly-Choque, M., Hart, C., Robinson, C., Nelson, L., & Olsen, S. (1996). Overt and relational aggression on the playground: Correspondence among different informants. *Journal of Research in Childhood Education*, **11**, 47–67.

Nagin, D., & Tremblay, R. (1999). Trajectories of boys' physical aggression, opposition, and hyperactivity on the path to physically violent and nonviolent juvenile delinquency. *Child Development*, **70**, 1181–1196.

NICHD Early Child Care Research Network. (1998). Early child care and self-control: Compliance and behavior problems at twenty-four and thirty-six months. *Child Development*, **69**, 1145–1170.

NICHD Early Child Care Research Network. (2003). Does the amount of time spent in child care predict socioemotional adjustment during the transition to kindergarten. *Child Development*, **74**, 976–1005.

Olweus, D. (1979). Stability of aggression reaction patterns in males: A review. *Psychological Bulletin*, **86**, 852–857.

Sameroff, A. (1996). Democratic and Republican models of development: Paradigms or perspectives. American Psychological Association Presidential Address. Toronto,

Canada. Reprinted in the Fall, August 1996, Division 7 Newsletter (Developmental Psychology).

Sameroff, A., Seifer, R., Baldwin, A., & Baldwin, C. (1993). Stability of intelligence from preschool to adolescence. *Child Development*, **64**, 80–97.

Shaw, D., Gilliom, M., Ingoldsby, E., & Nagin, D. (2003). Trajectories leading to school-age conduct problems. *Developmental Psychology*, **39**, 189–200.

Sutton, J., Smith, P., & Swettenham, J. (1999). Bullying and "theory of mind": A critique of the "social skills deficit" view of anti-social behaviour. *Social Development*, **8**, 117–127.

Silverstein, L. (1991). Transforming the debate about child care and maternal employment. *American Psychologist*, **46**, 1025–1032.

Tremblay, R. (2000). The development of aggressive behavior during childhood: What have we learned in the past century? *International Journal of Behavioral Development*, **24**, 129–141.

Underwood, M., Galen, B., & Paquette, J. (2001). Top ten challenges for understanding gender and aggression in children: Why can't we all just get along? *Social Development*, **10**, 248–266.

CONTRIBUTORS

This study was directed by a Steering Committee and supported by the National Institute of Child Health and Human Development (NICHD) through a cooperative agreement (U10), which calls for scientific collaboration between the grantees and the NICHD staff. Alphabetically listed participating investigators are: Virginia Allhusen, University of California, Irvine; Jay Belsky, Birkbeck College, University of London; Cathryn Booth-LaForce, University of Washington; Robert Bradley, University of Arkansas, Little Rock; Celia A. Brownell, University of Pittsburgh; Margaret Burchinal, University of North Carolina, Chapel Hill; Susan B. Campbell, University of Pittsburgh; K. Alison Clarke-Stewart, University of California, Irvine; Martha Cox, University of North Carolina, Chapel Hill; Sarah L. Friedman, NICHD; Aletha Huston, University of Texas, Austin; Jean F. Kelly, University of Washington; Bonnie Knoke, Research Triangle Institute; Kathleen McCartney, Harvard University; Marion O'Brien, University of North Carolina at Greensboro; Margaret Tresch Owen, University of Texas, Dallas; Ross Parke, University of California, Riverside; Robert Pianta, University of Virginia; Michele Poe, University of North Carolina, Chapel Hill; Susan Spieker, University of Washington; Deborah Lowe Vandell, University of Wisconsin, Madison; and Marsha Weinraub, Temple University.

William F. Arsenio (Ph.D., 1986, Stanford University) is Associate Professor and Program Director of Developmental Psychology at Ferkauf Graduate School of Psychology, Yeshiva University. His research addresses how children's and adolescents' emotion recognition and affect-event knowledge is related to social competence as well as risk for psychopathology. Much of this work focuses on affective contributors to children's moral development and aggressive tendencies.

STATEMENT OF EDITORIAL POLICY

The *Monographs* series is devoted to publishing developmental research that generates authoritative new findings and uses these to foster fresh, better integrated, or more coherent perspectives on major developmental issues, problems, and controversies. The significance of the work in extending developmental theory and contributing definitive empirical information in support of a major conceptual advance is the most critical editorial consideration. Along with advancing knowledge on specialized topics, the series aims to enhance cross-fertilization among developmental disciplines and developmental sub fields. Therefore, clarity of the links between the specific issues under study and questions relating to general developmental processes is important. These links, as well as the manuscript as a whole, must be as clear to the general reader as to the specialist. The selection of manuscripts for editorial consideration, and the shaping of manuscripts through reviews-and-revisions, are processes dedicated to actualizing these ideals as closely as possible.

Typically *Monographs* entail programmatic large-scale investigations; sets of programmatic interlocking studies; or—in some cases—smaller studies with highly definitive and theoretically significant empirical findings. Multi-authored sets of studies that center on the same underlying question can also be appropriate; a critical requirement here is that all studies address common issues, and that the contribution arising from the set as a whole be unique, substantial, and well integrated. The needs of integration preclude having individual chapters identified by individual authors. In general, irrespective of how it may be framed, any work that is judged to significantly extend developmental thinking will be taken under editorial consideration.

To be considered, submissions should meet the editorial goals of *Monographs* and should be no briefer than a minimum of 80 pages (including references and tables). There is an upper limit of 175–200 pages. In exceptional circumstances this upper limit may be modified. (Please submit four copies.) Because a *Monograph* is inevitable lengthy and usually substantively complex, it is particularly important that the text be well organized and written in clear, precise, and literate English. Note, however, that authors from non-English-speaking countries should not be put off by this stricture. In accordance with the general aims of SRCD, this series is actively interested in promoting international exchange of developmental research. Neither membership in the Society nor affiliation with the academic discipline of psychology are relevant in considering a *Monographs* submission.

The corresponding author for any manuscript must, in the submission letter, warrant that all coauthors are in agreement with the content of the manuscript. The corresponding author also is responsible for informing all coauthors, in a timely manner, of manuscript submission, editorial decisions, reviews received, and any revisions recommended. Before publication, the corresponding author also must warrant in the submission letter that the study has been conducted according to the ethical guidelines of the Society for Research in Child Development.

Potential authors who may be unsure whether the manuscript they are planning would make an appropriate submission are invited to draft an outline of what they propose, and send it to the Editor for assessment. This mechanism, as well as a more detailed description of all editorial policies, evaluation process, and format requirements can be found at the Editorial Office web site (http://astro.temple.edu/-overton/monosrcd.html) or by contacting the Editor, Wills F. Overton, Temple University-Psychology, 1701 North 13th St. – Rm 567, Philadelphia, PA 19122-6085 (e-mail: monosrcd@temple.edu) (telephone: 1-215-204-7360).

Monographs of the Society for Research in Child Development (ISSN 0037-976X), one of two publications of Society of Research in Child Development, is published three times a year by Blackwell Publishing, Inc., with offices at 350 Main Street, Malden, MA 02148, USA, and 9600 Garsington Road, Oxford OX4 2XG, UK. Call US (800) 835-6770 or (781) 388-8206, UK +44 (0) 1865 778315; fax US (781) 388-8232, UK +44 (0) 1865 471775; e-mail US subscrip@bos.blackwellpublishing.com, UK customerservices@oxon.blackwellpublishing. com. A subscription to *Monographs of the SRCD* comes with a subscription to *Child Development* (published bimonthly).

INFORMATION FOR SUBSCRIBERS For new orders, renewals, sample copy requests, claims, change of address, and all other subscription correspondence, please contact the Journals Subscription Department at your nearest Blackwell office.

INSTITUTIONAL PREMIUM RATES* FOR MONOGRAPHS OF THE SRCD/CHILD DEVELOPMENT 2004 The Americas $420, Rest of World £298. Customers in Canada should add 7% GST to The Americas price or provide evidence of entitlement to exemption. Customers in the UK and EU should add VAT at 5% or provide a VAT registration number or evidence of entitlement to exemption.

*Includes print plus premium online access to the current and all available backfiles. Print and online-only rates are also available. For more information about Blackwell Publishing journals, including online access information, terms and conditions, and other pricing options, please visit www.blackwellpublishing.com or contact our customer service department, tel: (800) 835-6770 or (781) 388-8206 (US office); +44 (0)1865 778315 (UK office).

BACK ISSUES Back issues are available from the publisher at the current single issue rate.

MICROFORM The journal is available on microfilm. For microfilm service, address inquiries to ProQuest Information and Learning, 300 North Zeeb Road, Ann Arbor, MI 48106-1346, USA. Bell and Howell Serials Customer Service Department: (800) 521-0600 × 2873.

ADVERTISING For information and rates, please visit the journal's website at www.blackwellpublishing.com/MONO email: blackwellads@aidcvt.com, or contact Faith Elliott, Blackwell Advertising Representative, 50 Winter Sport Lane, PO Box 80, Williston, VT 05495. Phone: 800-866-1684 or Fax: 802-864-7749.

MAILING Journal is mailed Standard Rate. Mailing to rest of world by Deutsche Post Global Mail. Canadian mail is sent by Canadian publications mail agreement number 40573520. Postmaster: Send all address changes to Monographs of the Societey for Research in Child Development, Blackwell Publishing Inc., Journals Subscription Department, 350 Main St., Malden, MA 02148-5018.

Sign up to receive Blackwell *Synergy* free e-mail alerts with complete *Monographs of the SRCD* tables of contents and quick links to article abstracts from the most current issue. Simply go to www.blackwell-synergy.com, select the journal from the list of journals, and click on "Sign-up" for FREE email table of contents alerts.

CURRENT